National Real Estate Exam Prep for Salespersons:
Study Guide and Full-length Practice Exams

Study More Efficiently

Bova Books LLC
BovaBooks@gmail.com

Thank you for your Purchase!

We are available for full support of your studies for any questions or comments you may have. Email us at:

BovaBooks@gmail.com

Table of Contents   Page #

National Exam Content Outline for Salespersons

I. REAL PROPERTY CHARACTERISTICS, LEGAL DESCRIPTIONS, AND PROPERTY USE (9)

A. Real property vs. personal property
1. Fixtures, trade fixtures, emblements
2. Attachment, severance, and bill of sale

B. Characteristics of real property
1. Economic characteristics
2. Physical characteristics

C. Legal descriptions
1. Methods used to describe real property
2. Survey

D. Public and private land use controls – encumbrances
1. Public controls – governmental powers
   a. Police power, eminent domain, taxation, escheat
   b. Zoning ordinances
2. Private controls, restrictions, and encroachments
   a. Covenants, conditions, and restrictions (CC&Rs), HOAs
   b. Easements
   c. Licenses and encroachments

II. FORMS OF OWNERSHIP, TRANSFER, AND RECORDING OF TITLE (8)

A. Ownership, estates, rights, and interests
1. Forms of ownership
2. Freehold estate
   a. Fee simple absolute
   b. Fee simple defeasible, determinable, and condition subsequent
   c. Life estate
   d. Bundle of rights
3. Leasehold estates and types of leases
   a. Estate for years and from period to period (periodic estate)
   b. Estate at will and estate at sufferance
   c. Gross, net, and percentage leases
4. Liens and lien priority
5. Surface and sub-surface rights

B. Deed, title, transfer of title, and recording of title
1. Elements of a valid deed
2. Types of deeds
3. Title transfer

    a. Voluntary alienation
    b. Involuntary alienation
   4. Recording the title
    a. Constructive and actual notice
    b. Title abstract and chain of title
    c. Marketable title and cloud on title
    d. Attorney title opinion, quiet title lawsuit, and title insurance

III. PROPERTY VALUE AND APPRAISAL (11)

 A. Concept of value
   1. Market value vs. market price
   2. Characteristics of value
   3. Principles of value
 B. Appraisal process
   1. Purpose and steps to an appraisal
   2. Federal oversight of the appraisal process
 C. Methods of estimating value and Broker Price Opinions (BPO)
   1. Sales comparison approach (market data)
   2. Cost approach
    a. Improvements and depreciation
    b. Physical deterioration, functional, and economic obsolescence
    c. Reproduction or replacement costs
   3. Income approach
   4. Gross rent and gross income multipliers
   5. Comparative Market Analysis (CMA)
   6. Broker Price Opinion (BPO)
   7. Assessed value and tax implications

IV. REAL ESTATE CONTRACTS AND AGENCY (16)

 A. Types of contracts
   1. Express vs. implied
   2. Unilateral vs. bilateral
 B. Required elements of a valid contract
 C. Contract performance
   1. Executed vs. executory
   2. Valid vs. void
   3. Voidable vs. unenforceable
   4. Breach of contract, rescission, and termination
   5. Liquidated, punitive, or compensatory damages
   6. Statute of Frauds

7. Time is of the essence

D. Sales contract

    1. Offer and counteroffer

    2. Earnest money and liquidated damages

    3. Equitable title

    4. Contingencies

    5. Disputes and breach of contract

    6. Option contract and installment sales contract

E. Types of agency and licensee-client relationships

F. Creation and termination of agency

G. Licensee obligations to parties of a transaction

V. REAL ESTATE PRACTICE (14)

A. Responsibilities of broker

    1. Practicing within scope of expertise

    2. Unauthorized practice of law

B. Brokerage agreements between the broker and principal (seller, buyer, landlord, or tenant)

    1. Seller representation – Types of listing agreements

        a. Exclusive right-to-sell and exclusive agency listing

        b. Non-exclusive or open listing

        c. Net listing (conflict of interest)

        d. Multiple listing service (MLS)

    2. Buyer representation

    3. Property management agreement

        a. Accounting for funds

        b. Property maintenance

        c. Leasing property

        d. Collecting rents and security deposits

    4. Termination of agreements

    5. Services, fees, and compensation

C. Fair Housing

    1. Equal opportunity in housing

    2. Protected classes

    3. Fair housing laws

    4. Illegal practices, enforcement, and penalties

    5. Prohibited advertising

    6. Housing and Urban Development (HUD)

    7. Americans with Disabilities Act (ADA)

D. Risk management

    1. Supervision

    2. Compliance with federal regulations; including Privacy and Do Not Contact

3. Vicarious liability

4. Antitrust laws

5. Fraud and misrepresentation

6. Types of insurance

    a. Errors and Omissions

    b. General Liability

VI. PROPERTY DISCLOSURES AND ENVIRONMENTAL ISSUES (8)

A. Property conditions and environmental issues

1. Hazardous substances

    a. Lead-based paint

    b. Asbestos, radon, and mold

    c. Groundwater contamination and underground storage tanks

    d. Waste disposal sites and brownfields

    e. Flood plains, flood zones, and flood insurance

2. Clean Air and Water Acts

3. Environmental Protection Agency (EPA)

    a. Comprehensive Environmental Response, Compensation, and Liability Act (CERCLA)

    b. Superfund Amendment and Reauthorization Act (SARA)

    c. Environmental site assessments (including Phase I and II studies) and impact statements

    d. Wetlands protection

B. Disclosure obligations and liability

VII. FINANCING AND SETTLEMENT (7)

A. Financing concepts and components

1. Methods of financing

    a. Mortgage financing – conventional and non-conventional loans

    b. Seller financing – land contract/contract for deed

2. Lien theory vs. title theory and deed of trust

3. Sources of financing (primary and secondary mortgage markets, and seller financing)

4. Types of loans and loan programs

5. Mortgage clauses

B. Lender Requirements

1. FHA requirements

2. VA requirements

3. Buyer qualification and Loan to Value (LTV)

4. Hazard and flood insurance

5. Private mortgage insurance (PMI) and mortgage insurance premium (MIP)

C. Federal Financing Regulations and Regulatory Bodies

    1. Truth-in-Lending and Regulation Z

    2. TILA-RESPA Integrated Disclosures (TRID)

        a. Consumer Financial Protection Bureau (CFPB)

        b. Loan Estimate (LE)

        c. Closing Disclosure (CD)

    3. Real Estate Settlement Procedures Act (RESPA)

        a. Referrals

        b. Rebates

    4. Equal Credit Opportunity Act (ECOA)

    5. Mortgage fraud and predatory lending

D. Settlement and closing the transaction

VIII. REAL ESTATE MATH CALCULATIONS (7)

A. Property area calculations

    1. Square footage

    2. Acreage total

B. Property valuation

    1. Comparative Market Analysis (CMA)

    2. Net Operating Income (NOI)

    3. Capitalization rate

    4. Equity in property

    5. Establishing a listing price

    6. Assessed value and property taxes

C. Commission/compensation

D. Loan financing costs

    1. Interest

    2. Loan to Value (LTV)

    3. Fees

    4. Amortization, discount points, and prepayment penalties

E. Settlement and closing costs

    1. Purchase price and down payment

    2. Monthly mortgage calculations- principal, interest, taxes, and insurance (PITI)

    3. Net to the seller

    4. Cost to the buyer

    5. Prorated items

    6. Debits and credits

    7. Transfer tax and recording fee

F. Investment

    1. Return on investment

2. Appreciation
3. Depreciation
4. Tax implications on investment
G. Property management calculations
    1. Property management and budget calculations
    2. Tenancy and rental calculations

National Exam Study Guide

I. REAL PROPERTY CHARACTERISTICS, LEGAL DESCRIPTIONS, AND PROPERTY USE (9)

Real estate is defined as an identified piece of land along with any permeant improvements attached to the land either man-made or natural. Properties can be classified as one of the following:

- **Residential real estate**: A property used for residential purposes.
- **Commercial real estate**: A property used exclusively for business purposes.
- **Industrial real estate**: Any property used for manufacturing, production, distribution, storage, and research and development.
- **Land**: Includes undeveloped property, vacant land, and agricultural land
- **Special purpose**: Property used by and for the public. This may include cemeteries, government buildings, libraries, parks, places of worship, and schools.

A. Real property vs. personal property

All property can be either real or personal. To determine which category a piece of property falls under depends on whether an individual can physically move it.

Real property is land or things attached to land which cannot be moved. Trees or plants that grow on land can also be considered real property unless they require routine cultivation or labor, such as crops.

There are two categories of personal property: chattels and intangibles. Chattels refer to all types of tangible property such as furniture or clothing. Some chattels are attached to the land and can become a part of real property, which are known as fixtures. Intangibles are forms of personal property that are not tangible. This means that the property cannot be touched or seen. This includes intellectual property, licenses, insurance policies, and investments such as stocks or bonds.

1. Fixtures, trade fixtures, emblements

In real estate, any item that is fastened or attached to the property is considered a fixture. Fixtures are part of the property and should be included as a part of the sale of the property. A fixture that a seller wants to keep should be removed before the showing of the property. For example, if a microwave is removed by the seller after a buyer has seen it, it should be replaced with another microwave that is of equal value.

There are several criteria that can be used to classify whether a property is a fixture or not. These include:

- **How is the item attached:** Anything permanently attached to the wall, floor, or ceiling with nails, screws, glue, or others is likely a fixture. Examples include lights, ceiling fans, wall sconces, TV mounts, shelves, etc.
- **Inclusion of the item with the construction of the property.** If an item was specifically built and permanently installed in the home to be used with the property, it shall be considered a fixture. Examples include carpeting, floor planks, and built-in cabinets.
- **Agreement between the buyer and seller.** The safest way to determine what shall be considered a fixture is to include all items in the purchase agreement. This will remove any discrepancy and confusion between the buyer and seller.

Trade fixtures are pieces of property that a tenant affixes to a leased building or land for the purpose of conducting business. This may include a display counter, a bar, or equipment for the purposes of moving products. The trade fixtures shall still be removable otherwise it becomes the property of the owner.

Emblements are crops grown on a piece of property leased to a tenant. The crops are the property of the person who provided labor to grow them, regardless of who owns the property.

2. Attachment, severance, and bill of sale

Attachments are anything attached to the property. They can be classified as either natural or man-made:

Natural attachments are items that are part of the land and occur naturally. This includes things like trees, shrubs, streams, and plants that are meant to be permanent. These are part of the real property and belong to the land.

Man-made attachments are items that were added to the land and meant to be permanent or long-term. This includes the home itself and any additional attachments such as fences, sidewalks, wells, or swimming pools.

Severance is the opposite of attachment. Severance is removing an object that is attached to the land. Once it is removed, it can now be classified as personal property.

A Bill of Sale is proof of purchase when buying or selling an item. This is more common with larger or higher-priced items such as vehicles or animals, but can also be obtained with other items which can be simply saving the receipt from purchase. The elements of a bill of sale include:

- Date of purchase
- Name and address of the seller and buyer
- Amount paid for the transfer of ownership
- Description of the assets being transferred

- Guarantee that the item is free from all claims and offsets
- Representations or warranties
- Signatures of the seller, of the buyer, and a notary public

B. Characteristics of real property

1. Economic characteristics

Land has some distinct economic characteristics that influence its value as an investment:

- **Scarcity**: The relative availability of property in relation to demand.
- **Improvements**: Any additions or changes to the land or a building that affects the property's value is called an improvement.
- **Permanence of investment**: Once work is performed on the land, there is a portion of the work that is considered to have permanent value. Some improvements that have permanence include items such as drainage, electricity, water, and sewer systems.
- **Location or area preference**: Location is fixed for a property. However, the location may become more or less desirable based on external factors.

2. Physical characteristics

Land has three distinct physical characteristics:

1. **Immobility**: While the land can be manipulated such as excavation or adding fill, the property in question cannot be moved.
2. **Indestructibility**: Similarly, to immobility, while the land can be manipulated, it cannot be completely destroyed.
3. **Uniqueness**: No two parcels of land can be exactly the same.

C. Legal descriptions

1. Methods used to describe real property

There are 3 common methods that can be used to determine the exact location and boundaries of a parcel of land:

1. Metes-and-bounds
2. Rectangular survey
3. Lot and block

Metes-and-bounds descriptions have been used for a long time. This method establishes a point of beginning (POB). Then metes are determined which are boundary lines that enclose an area. This area is called bounds. Starting at the POB, the length and angle of each mete are described from the previous boundary. This description and process are continued until the mete reaches the point of end (POE), which is the same as the point of beginning to create a closed shape. The location of the POB must be established by a monument or landmark, and It can be an artificial or natural object.

The rectangular survey system determines locations by using a rectangular coordinate system that consists of principal meridians (longitude) that are north and south and baselines that run east and west (latitude). Meridians and baselines divide the land into quadrangles, which are squares of land with each side measuring 24 miles. The quadrangles are further subdivided into 16 townships, with each side of a township measuring 6 miles and covering an area of 36 square miles. Townships are further subdivided into 36 1-square mile sections, with each section equal to 640 acres. The rectangular survey system breaks down into a mete-and-bounds description to describe small parcels of land.

The lot-and-block system is where parcels of land are identified by a lot number or letter and the block, or subdivision plat, in which the lot is located. The block itself is located by using either the metes-and-bounds system or the rectangular survey system.

2. Survey

A property survey confirms or determines a property's boundary lines and the specifics of any other restrictions or easements for the property. Different states have different laws and some may require a property line survey for the purchase of real estate. Property surveys can be used to establish the following items:

- Legal boundaries: Determines the exact boundaries of the property. Helps to avoid or identify an encroachment which is when a neighbor builds something that intrudes on property they do not own.
- Easements: A property survey will reveal any easements on the property that may allow access to others on a specific property.
- Elevation: Determining elevations on a property may help in understanding the need for flood insurance or the extent of modifications to the property if needed or desired.
- Hazard Areas: A survey can identify any areas which may not be able to be built on such as wetlands or that may have identified hazards such as unstable conditions.

D. Public and private land use controls – encumbrances

1. Public controls – governmental powers

a. Police power, eminent domain, taxation, escheat

Police power gives the government the right to enact regulations for the health, safety, and welfare of the public. It is important to note that police power can be enforced without the need for any compensation. Some examples of areas of violation that would warrant the use of police power include:

- Building codes
- Zoning laws
- Safety regulations
- Rights of tenants and landlords
- Environmental regulations and control
- Right to damage property for the best public interest

Eminent domain is the right of the government to take or use private property for public use. This must include what is determined to be fair compensation. This applies to airspace, land, and contract rights to intellectual property. The legal debate surrounding the unfair invoking of eminent domain is called inverse condemnation. Private landowners who lose their home or land due to eminent domain must be paid just compensation. This can be debated but this is generally based on how much the landowner might expect to get in fair market value. The planners of a project who exercise eminent domain will provide an offer to the landowner. If the offer is not accepted, the dispute will go to a condemnation process. In this, the property owner will offer their own property valuation and a determination will be made.

Property Taxation: Property taxes are imposed on the owner by the state to pay for local governmental functions just as any other taxes. Not all states have property taxes but those who do are most often determined by an assessed value and a millage rate.

Escheat: The right of the government to take ownership of estate assets or unclaimed property. This is common when an individual dies with no will and no heirs. The escheatment process is revocable if a legitimate heir is discovered or revealed but individual states may have a statute of limitations on the amount of time that allows for a reversal of government ownership.

b. Zoning ordinances

Zoning ordinances define how property in specific geographic zones can be used. For example, they may regulate lot size, placement, density, and the height of structures. For example, a municipality may restrict the minimum lot size for a home to be built on to maintain a specific character of a neighborhood.

2. Private controls, restrictions, and encroachments

a. Covenants, conditions, and restrictions (CC&Rs), HOAs

Homes purchased that are a part of a homeowners' association (HOA) are subject to rules of the HOA community. These rules are described in a Declaration of Covenants, Conditions, and Restrictions (CC&Rs). The CC&Rs describe the requirements and limitations of what an individual can do with the property. Some common CC&R restrictions and requirements include but are not limited to:

- Property maintenance.
- Restrictions on changes to the look or decoration of a home
- Pet restrictions
- Parking restrictions

Penalties for Violating the CC&Rs may include:

- Fines
- Suspension of your privileges such as common areas
- Forced compliance
- Legal action

b. Easements

An easement is the granting of rights to use or access land by someone other than the owner. Easements are important to be made aware of during a purchase transaction as there can be a misrepresentation of the acceptable use of a piece of land by other parties. Easements can be both permanent or temporary.

c. Licenses and encroachments

An encroachment is when a property owner violates the established property rights agreed to with the neighbors. This is often done by building on or extending a structure to the neighbor's property. This may be done intentionally or not. Encroachments may require a survey to be performed to determine the exact location of property boundaries. An agreed upon easement may be a solution to allow a property owner specific rights to another property in exchange for some compensation.

II. FORMS OF OWNERSHIP, TRANSFER, AND RECORDING OF TITLE (8)

A. Ownership, estates, rights, and interests

1. Forms of ownership

Real estate ownership can take several forms. The most common ways of title holding are:

- **Sole ownership:** Property owned by an individual or entity legally capable of holding the title. This includes property held by a single person or married people who hold property apart from their spouse. This also includes businesses that invest in or use real estate.
- **Joint tenancy:** For two or more people owning real estate jointly. This comes with equal rights. If one of the partners dies, their rights of ownership pass to the surviving tenant(s) through a legal relationship known as a right of survivorship.
- **Tenancy in common:** Where two or more persons hold title to real estate jointly, with equal or unequal percentages of ownership. Despite the uneven ownership, all aspects of the property are shared by the people named on the title. The interest percentage determines the financial ownership of the real estate. Unlike joint tenancy, tenants in common hold title individually for their respective portion of the property and can dispose of or encumber it at will.
- **Tenants by entirety:** This is for legally married couples only. The ownership of the property is under the assumption that the couple is one person for legal purposes. This allows the transfer of property at death to not require any legal process or documents, avoiding the need for the property to be transferred under a will.
- **Community property:** Joint ownership by a husband and wife during their marriage in which each spouse owns everything equally, regardless of who earned or spent the money. Thus, each spouse gets an equal division of real estate property in the event of divorce or death. This is not available in all states.

2. Freehold estate

a. Fee simple absolute

Fee simple absolute is an interest in property a person will receive when they either buy land or receive land as a gift. The interest is absolute because the interest will not end based on the occurrence of an event or condition.

b. Fee simple defeasible, determinable, and condition subsequent

Fee Simple Defeasible: A fee simple that is not entirely absolute and can end with the violation of a condition. If the identified condition is never violated, the property will be owned indefinitely and a future interest will never vest. A fee simple defeasible can be one of the following types:

- **Fee Simple Determinable**: A fee simple interest in property that is terminated automatically upon the occurrence or non-occurrence of an event or condition. If the condition is violated, the property will automatically shift back to the grantor without having to take any further action.
- **Fee Simple Subject to a Condition Subsequent**: A fee simple interest that can be terminated at the will of a future interest holder upon the occurrence or non-occurrence of an event or condition. In other words, if the condition is violated, the grantor has the choice of action.
- **Fee Simple Subject to Executory Limitation:** A fee simple defeasible which confers a future property interest in a third party, and not the original owner.

Fee Tail: An interest in land that is inheritable by and transferable to only lineal descendants of the original grantee.

c. Life estate

A life estate is property that an individual owns only through the duration of their lifetime. It is also referred to as a tenant for life and life tenant. It also prevents the beneficiary from selling the property that produces the income before the beneficiary's death. But the estate cannot continue beyond the life of the beneficiary.

d. Bundle of rights

Bundle of rights is a term for the set of legal privileges that is generally afforded to a real estate buyer with the transfer of the title. The bundle includes the following:

The right of possession: The title holder is the legal owner of the property.

The right of control: The title holder can use the property in any way that is not illegal.

The right of exclusion: Allows the titleholder to limit who may enter the property.

The right of enjoyment: Asserts the title holder's right to participate in any activities he finds pleasurable while on the property as long as the activities are legal.

The right of disposition: Protects the title holder's right to transfer ownership, permanently or temporarily, to another party.

3. Leasehold estates and types of leases

a. Estate for years and from period to period (periodic estate)

An estate for years is a lease with an established beginning and end date. At the end of the established time period, the tenant is expected to vacate the property, and notice is not required.

A periodic estate has no specific ending date for a lease, but there is a stipulated term. This is also known as a periodic tenancy or estate from period to period. The landlord and tenant agree to certain arrangements for these periods but do not specify an ending date. Since no ending date is specified, notice per the agreement must be given for termination and vacancy.

b. Estate at will and estate at sufferance

Estate at will is where a tenant occupies a property with the consent of the owner but without a formal written contract or lease. The amount of time is not predetermined and provides both the landlord and the tenant with flexibility in the agreement. This is a common arrangement between individuals who are friends or family. The agreement is covered under state law and legal protections exist despite the lack of a written contract. For instance:

- The landlord must provide a safe environment.
- The landlord must provide notice before entering the property.

The tenant also has to meet certain requirements by law such as:

- On time rent payments
- Any rules they have agreed to with the landlord orally or previously.
- The tenant is responsible for any damages beyond normal wear and tear

Estate at sufferance is an agreement in which a tenant is legally permitted to live on a property after a lease term has expired but before the landlord has provided notice to vacate. If an estate at sufferance occurs, the original lease conditions still apply.

c. Gross, net, and percentage leases

A gross lease is one that includes all costs a tenant might incur during their stay. In addition to rent, this includes taxes, insurance, utilities, and any others. Gross leases are undesirable to the landlord and not as common since there is an uncertainty in the total use of utilities.

In a net lease, the tenant is responsible for some or all costs associated such as utilities, maintenance, insurance, and others. There are three types of net leases:

- Single: The tenant pays rent plus property taxes.
- Double: The tenant pays rent plus property taxes and insurance.
- Triple: The tenant pays for rent plus property taxes, insurance, and maintenance.

A percentage lease is an agreement with commercial tenants in which there is a requirement to pay the landlord a fixed percentage of gross revenue earned from business conducted at the property. This is in addition to the base rent. Typically, the base will be reduced in comparison to a comparable residential-only property.

4. Liens and lien priority

Liens are claims against a property to ensure an existing debt is paid. If money is owed, the creditor is able to impose the debt on the property and that debt is now tied to the value of the property as collateral. If the debt is not paid, the creditor has a claim to the value of the property to satisfy the debt. Some common instances of liens include:

- Home equity loans
- Delinquent tax payments

The title insurance covers both the lender and the borrower from loss or damages resulting from the property title. This may be existing liens or encumbrances that will result in financial attention. Unlike typical insurance, this insurance covers past events that have not yet been uncovered.

Priority in the case of multiple mortgages is determined by a subordination agreement to establish the hierarchy of loans. Junior liens are established and are only paid after the primary loans have been paid in the case of default.

A lien is a financial stake in an asset. Junior liens are loans that use an existing asset as collateral that already has an existing loan. For mortgages, this is often a home equity loan with a first mortgage that has yet to be fully paid off. There is a hierarchy of liens that must be paid off in order of seniority. The original mortgage must be paid off first and then any junior liens thereafter in order of the oldest being paid off first.

Subordinate loans, sometimes referred to as subordinated debts, are similar to the concept of junior liens. A subordinate loan ranks below the primary loan and will not be paid off in the event of default until the loans higher in ranking are paid first. Due to this, there is a significant amount more risk if a loan is subordinate and terms may be unfavorable.

5. Surface and sub-surface rights

Surface rights include ownership to the owner for use of everything above the ground within the property boundaries. This includes structures, buildings, fences, trees, and water access rights.

Subsurface rights refer to the ownership of the land below a property's surface. The property owner generally has exclusive rights to the soil, minerals, and any other materials found underneath the land. If there are any deviations to this, it must be disclosed in the title deed at the time of purchase. If no restrictions are indicated, it can be assumed the buyer full subsurface rights to the property unless this is not stipulated under state law. There are scenarios where land ownership may be separated. Subsurface rights can be valuable if there is the presence of oil, natural gas, or minerals.

B. Deed, title, transfer of title, and recording of title

1. Elements of a valid deed

In order for a deed to be valid and legally enforceable, the deed must meet the following requirements:

- The deed must be in writing.
- The deed must convey title to real property.
- Notarized Signature by the grantor.
- There must be an identified grantor and grantee.
- It must be determined that the grantor is willing and competent to enter into the agreement.
- There must be a legal description of the property.
- The deed should be recorded for legal notice purposes to establish priority and the sequence of ownership.
- The grantee must accept the deed.

2. Types of deeds

Types of deeds include:

General Warranty Deed: A common deed that contains three guarantees:

- The grantor owns the title free and clear of any defects from the time the grantor owned the property back to prior ownership of the property.
- There are no liens or encumbrances other than stated in the deed.
- The grantor will defend the title of the property against third-party claims.

Grant Deed: Similar to warranty deeds but only contains the following two guarantees:

- The property has not been sold to anyone else.
- There are no encumbrances other than those disclosed by the seller

Quitclaim Deed: Conveys an interest of the grantor in the property to another party. There are no warranties made by the grantor that the title is good or that the property is free from liens or encumbrances. Commonly used to transfer property interests from one spouse to another.

Special or Limited Warranty Deed: The grantor only warrants any title defect from the time the grantor took possession of the property, but not prior.

Fiduciary Deed: Used when there is a guardianship or conservatorship involving real property transfer. The trustee or executor of the estate has the authority to sell property that belongs to the estate.

Release Deed: Releases the property from the original lien placed on the property.

Tax Deed: Tax deeds are issued by municipalities when a property is sold for back taxes.

Bargain and Sale Deed: Guarantees that the grantor has the title, but does not guarantee that the title is free of defects.

Gift Deed: Included in the transfer of real estate between relatives where no exchange of money has taken place.

Deed in Lieu of Foreclosure: Used when a borrower is in default on their mortgage to avoid foreclosure. The lender receives the deed from the borrower.

3. Title transfer

a. Voluntary alienation

Voluntary alienation in real estate is the peaceful transfer of the residency rights or deed of a property between two parties. This does not require the use of extraneous legal measures. There is a clear agreement and understanding of transfer.

b. Involuntary alienation

Involuntary alienation is the acquisition of property against the wishes of the owner. This can occur in a number of different ways:

Adverse possession: An individual other than the owner uses a piece of property openly, publicly, and without the owner's consent for a specified period of time. If an individual wishes to successfully claim adverse possession they must exhibit the following:

- **Continuous use:** The claimant must have proof of continuous possession of the property or portion of the property.
- **Hostile takeover:** There must be no existing agreement between the parties. This may include a lease or easement.
- **Open and notorious possession:** The claim on the property is clear and obvious.
- **Actual possession:** The property is treated as if it is owned by the claimant. This may include maintenance or paying taxes.
- **Exclusive use:** Only the claimant uses the property.

Avulsion: The sudden loss of land by natural processes. This may occur by powerful natural events such as hurricanes, landslides, earthquakes, erosion, and others. Accretion is the opposite of avulsion which is the gaining of land by natural forces. These events may change the outline of property limits and therefore altering the ownership of property.

Eminent domain: The taking of land against an individual wishes by the government or other public agency for public purposes for fair compensation. This is covered in greater detail later.

Foreclosure: Loss of property due to a failure to meet the debt obligations of a mortgage. The lender can seize the property and force eviction which removes the property owner.

Short Sale: Loss of property due to failure to meet payment obligations but the lender agrees to have the house sold for a price that is less than the amount still owed on the mortgage. An agreement is made as to the responsibilities of any money owed after the sale of the home.

Forfeiture: Loss of property due to failure to meet obligations as stipulated on the deed.

Partitioning: The legal subdivision of a property between joint landowners who do not have an agreement on the use of the land.

4. Recording the title

a. Constructive and actual notice

The receipt of information is important for real estate transactions to ensure the buyer and the seller are fully aware of all information that is necessary to be disclosed. Information that is provided directly is called actual notice. There are two types of actual notice express and implied:

- **Express actual notice** is when an individual has been given notice about a property without the need to make any inference. This can be a direct statement written or orally.
- **Implied actual notice** is when an individual witnesses something that provided them with information about the property. No one has told the individual directly but it is reasonable to assume that the information or event provided the necessary notice.

Constructive notice is a legal assumption that an individual should have knowledge of an event or transaction that is printed in the public record. It can be assumed that if the information is available to the public, then the individual should be aware regardless of formal acknowledgment. This generally can apply to documents and guidelines released by organizations or announcements made in news outlets.

b. Title abstract and chain of title

Abstract of title is a record of the title history of a property. This documents the transactions for the property including transfers, liens, and legal actions that are connected to the property. This document ensures a clear title.

The **chain of title** traces the historical transfer of ownership from the current owner back to the original owner. The chain of title is much more detailed in the specifics of ownership than the abstract of title.

c. Marketable title and cloud on title

A **marketable title** is one that is free and clear of any defects or clouds that a reasonable buyer would find objectionable. This does not guarantee that the title is free of mistakes but that a court will legally force its acceptance by a buyer.

A **cloud on title** is any claim, or encumbrance that might invalidate a title to real property. Clouds on the title are typically discovered during a title search. Clouds on the title are resolved by initiating a quitclaim deed, which releases a person's interest in a property without stating the nature of the person's interests.

d. Attorney title opinion, quiet title lawsuit, and title insurance

An **opinion of title** is an attorney's legal opinion on the validity of the title deed to a parcel of property. A closing protection letter is also often included which is insurance that further verifies that the attorney who reviewed the title policy and issued the opinion of title assumes responsibility for any legal recourse that could arise due to erroneous reporting.

A **quiet title lawsuit** is a legal action that is intended to clarify ownership of a given property. The action is defined as quiet to avoid attempts from outside entities to acquire the property in question.

Title insurance protects lenders and buyers from financial loss due to defects in a title to a property. The claims may include back taxes, liens, and conflicting wills. A title insurance fee is often required as a part of closing costs for the buyer.

III. PROPERTY VALUE AND APPRAISAL (11)

A. Concept of value

1. Market value vs. market price

The market price of a home is the amount a willing and qualified buyer in the market will pay for the home if the seller is willing to accept it. In other words, it is the amount a home will sell for in an actual transaction or the sales price. This will be used as a benchmark for future valuations. The market price can be influenced by characteristics of individual preference that may drive the price up or down. For example, a buyer may put increased emphasis on a location to be near family and therefore willing to pay more than most buyers.

The market value is an opinion of what a property would sell for in a competitive market based on the characteristics of the property, the current local real estate market, and comparable properties. This is akin to the appraised value of the property.

2. Characteristics of value

Value is subjective but is determined by a number of characteristics that can influence the perception of an asset's value. These include:

Demand: The demand for a piece of real estate is determined by the amount of interest in that particular property. This may be influenced by an individual's specific desire to be in a specific location or the influx of many people who find the subject property desirable.

Utility: Utility is a measure of the usefulness of a property. Usefulness fills a need and therefore creates a desire for ownership. Each individual buyer has a minimum level of utility such as no less than three bedrooms, be near the ocean, or other specific features.

Scarcity: Scarcity is a measure of the availability of a specific product relative to the amount of demand. If too many houses are for sale, it is easier for buyers to find what they want and sellers will be more willing to compromise for their home to be chosen. Conversely, few available homes create more demand for the home giving the buyer less options.

Purchasing Power: Purchasing power is the ability of a buyer to afford the home. The more people that can afford the property, the more available buyers.

Transferability: Transferability in an asset can make it more desirable. For example, some portions of a home may have a transferable warranty such as a roof or other major aspects of a home. This feature makes it a more desirable purchase since the full value of the asset can be transferred.

3. Principles of value

1. Principle of Anticipation: Purchase of property for the anticipation of future benefits.

2. Principle of Demand, Supply, and Desire: The availability of assets and the desire for it affects the value.

3. Principle of Substitution: The value of a property can be properly estimated by an equally desirable substitute property. This is the basis of using comparable properties to determine value.

4. Principle of Balance: Principle of value invested having some increase in value. This applies to improvements such as a new bathroom increasing the value of a home.

5. Principle of Progression: The price of a property increases with an increased perceived value of a location.

6. Principle of Regression: This is the opposite of the progression principle. The price of a property decreases with a reduced perceived value of a site

B. Appraisal process

1. Purpose and steps to an appraisal

Appraisals are a third-party, independent evaluation of a home. They are always involved in a purchase transaction and are likely included in refinancing or other non-purchase transactions. The appraisal is necessary to ensure that the lender is not providing more money to the borrower for the loan than the asset is worth. This way in case of default, the asset can account for the remaining balance. If an appraisal comes in at less than the proposed transaction loan amount, then the transaction will not be processed unless the borrower provides a greater down payment. There are three types of appraisals which will be discussed in the following sections.

The ordering of an appraisal may come from the lender to ensure the value of the loan is acceptable in comparison to the fair market value. The borrower may choose the specific appraiser, but the appraisal must be approved by the lender.

Other scenarios for ordering an appraisal may include a seller for the purposes of setting a price before putting the home on the market or a homeowner looking to evaluate existing equity for a refinance loan. If these appraisals are to be used in a transaction, however, they must be approved by the lender.

2. Federal oversight of the appraisal process

A creditor must provide an applicant a copy of all appraisals and other written valuations developed in connection with an application for credit. A creditor shall provide a copy of each such appraisal or other written valuation promptly upon completion, or three business days prior to consummation of the transaction (for closed-end credit) or account opening (for open-end credit), whichever is earlier. An applicant may waive the timing requirement by written consent.

The Equal Credit Opportunity Act (ECOA) Valuations Rule provides requirements for a borrower's right to receive an appraisal. The borrower must be provided with a disclosure that includes the following:

- Notice of the right to receive a copy of an appraisal report.
- Requirement that the applicant's request must be in writing.
- The lender's mailing address.
- The requirement that the lender is required to send a copy of the appraisal report only if the applicant's request is received no more than 90 days after the lender has provided notice of action taken on the application under section 1002.9 of Regulation B or 90 days after the application is withdrawn.

The lender is required to send the right to receive a copy of the appraisal disclosure no more than 3 days from the date of application.

C. Methods of estimating value and Broker Price Opinions (BPO)

1. Sales comparison approach (market data)

The market approach is the most common of the appraisal types and is used for most purchase loans. The value of the home is determined by comparison to other properties with similar characteristics that have been sold in as recent of a timeframe as possible. The comparisons (referred to as "comps") are then evaluated by identifying the differences in certain characteristics such as square footage, age, lot size, home type, street type, and many others. Typically, a minimum of three comps are required and the most similar and most recent homes are chosen. At times, homes that are currently on the market are also used as a basis for comparison but will not hold as much weight as the sales. If possible, homes no more than a 1-mile radius away from the home shall be chosen and as well as no more than 1 year prior to the transaction.

Once the comps are evaluated in comparison to the home to be purchased, the prices of the sales are adjusted to represent a price of equal value. These values are then averaged and evaluated using some appraiser judgment to determine a fair market value of the home.

Choosing comparable properties does not have exact requirements but should be as close as possible in size, location, age, and other characteristics. The comparable homes should also be sold as recently as possible. Homes shall also not be sold longer than a year from the proposed transaction. In rural areas, a lower volume of sales may lead to an expansion of the requirements for the chosen comparable properties. The appraiser shall use sound judgment based on the market to choose the most appropriate homes.

2. Cost approach

For a building that is not frequently sold, the cost approach determines what the value of the property may be by assuming that a reasonable buyer would not pay more than for a comparable building on a comparable lot. Often this is most appropriate for buildings such as schools, hospitals, or government buildings that are not bought and sold frequently. To determine value as per the cost approach, the property's value is determined by the cost of land, plus total costs of construction, less depreciation:

$$Property\ Value = Cost\ of\ Construction + Cost\ of\ Land - Depreciation$$

a. Improvements and depreciation

Depreciation can be claimed from the home itself and any improvements to the home which have a lifespan. The home itself is spread out over a standard amount of time of 27.5 years. Any work performed on the home must be classified as either improvements or repairs. Improvements extend the useful life of the property. Examples are additions, remodeling, or replacements. For example, a roof classifies as an improvement and is to be depreciated over its lifespan of 20 years. The repairs are not depreciated over a lifespan.

b. Physical deterioration, functional, and economic obsolescence

Functional obsolescence is the reduction of a home's value due to outdated features that cannot be easily changed. For example, an old house with one bathroom in a neighborhood entirely with new homes that have multiple bathrooms. Functional obsolescence is often difficult to identify quantitatively because the impact on a buyer may be too great causing a greatly reduced level of interest.

Economic obsolescence is a loss of value of a property due to factors that are external to the property. The catalyst is outside of the control of the owner of the property and therefore the issue can most likely not be corrected. Some common examples include a change in aircraft flight patterns, increased crime rates, construction of a busy highway, construction of a landfill nearby, etc.

c. Reproduction or replacement costs

There are two methods for determining the cost of construction used in the determination of the cost approach:

- **Reproduction method**: Cost determined from an exact replica of the property including original materials.
- **Replacement method**: Cost of a new structure with newer materials, current construction methods and design.

3. Income approach

The income approach is a way of evaluating investment properties that will generate income. This is common for condo or apartment complexes where renters will reside. The approach involves calculating the Net Operating Income (NOI) which is the income generated divided by the capitalization rate:

$$NOI = \frac{Income}{Capitalization\ Rate}$$

The capitalization rate is a percentage representation of the expected income that can be generated from a property on a yearly basis if it is bought with a cash investment.

4. Gross rent and gross income multipliers

Gross rent is the total amount of rent that a tenant must pay as per an agreed upon lease. The gross rent is the cumulation of all monthly payments.

A gross income multiplier is an estimate of the value of an investment property. It is typically calculated by dividing the property's sale price by its estimated or provided gross annual rental income. It does not include the property's operating costs.

$$Gross\ Income\ Multiplier = \frac{Sale\ Price}{Gross\ Annual\ Rental\ Income}$$

5. Comparative Market Analysis (CMA)

A comparative market analysis (CMA) determines an estimate of a property's value by comparing characteristics of the home in the transaction to other recently sold and similar properties in the immediate area. Real estate agents often use CMA reports to assist sellers in determining listing prices for the properties they intend to sell or to determine what they may expect to make from a sale. Some of the identified comparable characteristics include location, age, size, construction, style, condition, and lot size.

Choosing comparable properties does not have exact requirements but should be as close as possible in identified characteristics. The comparable homes should also be sold as recently as possible. Homes shall also not be sold longer than a year from the proposed transaction. In rural areas, a lower volume of sales may lead to an expansion of the requirements for the chosen comparable properties. The appraiser shall use sound judgment based on the market to choose the most appropriate homes.

After comparable properties are selected, a dollar value needs to be assigned to each of the differences in characteristics. For instance, a difference in the number of bedrooms may account for $1000 per bedroom. Then the value of each home is adjusted accordingly due to the change in characteristics. After all adjustments are made, divide the adjusted price of each comparable property by its square footage to determine the sold price per square foot. Then get the average of the adjusted prices per square foot and multiply this average by the square feet of the subject property to find its CMA value.

6. Broker Price Opinion (BPO)

A broker price opinion (BPO) is an unofficial assessment of a property's potential market value based on expert judgment. A BPO is often based on qualitative and subjective factors such as neighborhood characteristics, curb appeal, and current market trends. A BPO is common to be performed for a potential client to get an estimate of what they may expect without having to initiate an official appraisal. A broker price opinion costs much less and can be done more quickly than an official appraisal of the property.

7. Assessed value and tax implications

The assessed value of a home is the amount assigned to a property to determine the local property taxes. It uses comparable home sales and inspections for its determination. Typically, the assessed value will be lower than the sales price or appraised value of the property. Tax assessors may do on-site value assessments to make adjustments as necessary to the value. The assessed value is a percentage of the fair market value and incorporates the overall quality of the property, property values, square footage, home features, and market conditions.

To calculate property tax, many states will use the millage rate equation:

$$Property\ Tax = \frac{Market\ Value\ of\ Property\ X\ Assessment\ Ratio\ X\ Millage\ Rate}{1000}$$

The millage rate is the tax rate applied to the assessed value. Millage rates are typically expressed per $1,000 with one mill representing $1 in tax for every $1,000.

IV. REAL ESTATE CONTRACTS AND AGENCY (16)

A. Types of contracts

1. Express vs. implied

An **express contract** is one in which the terms and conditions are clearly provided in the contract. This may be either verbally or in writing. Once an express contract has been established and agreed upon, an identical implied contract cannot exist.

An **implied contract** is still a legally-binding obligation but its terms are derived from actions, conduct, or circumstances of one or more parties in an agreement. It is still a legally binding agreement and as enforceable as an express contract. The implied contract requires no written or verbal confirmation.

2. Unilateral vs. bilateral

Unilateral contract: A contract in which one party makes an obligation to perform without receiving in return any express promise of performance from the other party. A unilateral contract contains a promise on one side, where as a bilateral contract contains promises on two sides.

Bilateral contract: A contract in which each party promises to perform an act in exchange for the other party's promise to perform. This is the typical type of real estate sales contract. If one party refuses to honor his or her promise and the other party is ready to perform, the nonperforming party is said to be in default. Neither party is liable to the other until there is first a performance.

B. Required elements of a valid contract

For a contract to be valid it must contain the following elements:

Offer and Acceptance: There must be a clear offer of some form whether it be goods, services, or property. Additionally, this offer must be clearly accepted by the receiving party.

Intention: It must be clear that the parties intended to enter into a legally binding contract. It can be generally assumed that the parties intended to enter into a contract. If a contract is discussed socially, the intention must be made clear.

Consideration: Some level of value must be exchanged for a contract to be binding. Consideration does not have to be at some minimum level of adequacy for the contract to be executed but some value must be present. For example, a home cannot be sold for nothing.

Legal capacity of the parties to act: Both parties must understand and be fully aware of what they are doing. Individuals with disabilities must not be taken advantage of.

Legality of the agreement: The purpose of the agreement cannot be in violation of the law.

C. Contract performance

1. Executed vs. executory

A contract is considered executed when all parties have met all the required obligations on the contract. The contract is considered complete at this point. This is not necessarily the act of signing the documents as there could be obligations beyond that point that must be met.

A contract is considered executory when there are obligations still outstanding on a contract. This may include any part of the contract including financing, agreed upon stipulations, title transfer, or any others.

2. Valid vs. void

A valid contract is one that can be met by all parties involved and executed without any illegal means. Valid contracts, once agreed to, are legally binding and enforceable by law.

A void contract is a formal agreement that is illegitimate and unenforceable from the moment it is created since it is not enforceable as it was originally written. This may be due to one of the involved parties being incapable of fully comprehending the stipulations of the contract. Additionally, this may be due to mental incapacity, minors entering into contracts, the presence of alcohol or drugs, or other instances. A contract that can be executed but includes illegal means is also considered a void contract.

3. Voidable vs. unenforceable

While a void contract is often considered not executable by design, a contract may be deemed voidable if the agreement is actionable, but the circumstances surrounding the agreement are questionable in nature. This includes agreements made where one party withheld information or intentionally provided inaccurate information. Failure to disclose items as required by law, or misrepresenting information, may render the contract voidable but doesn't automatically make it void. In instances when one party is allowed to cancel the contract because of the illegal or unfair (voidable) actions by the other party, the contract or agreement then becomes void.

An unenforceable contract will not hold up in a court of law and eliminates any obligations imposed on parties in the contract. A contract can be considered unenforceable if the elements of a valid contract are not met. Some common means of a contract becoming unenforceable may include:

- Party under duress
- Undue influence
- Lack of capacity
- False disclosure or information
- Mistakes or errors in the contract
- Events out of the control of the parties making the contract impossible to meet

4. Breach of contract, rescission, and termination

A breach of contract occurs when one party, in either a written or oral contract, fails to meet the terms of the agreement. The parties may work to resolve the issue among themselves, or it may escalate to be decided in a court of law. The different types of contract breaches include:

- Minor breach: the deliverable of the contract was ultimately received by the other party, but the party in breach failed to fulfill some part of their obligation.
- Material breach: An obligation is different from what was agreed to in the contract.
- Anticipatory: A party becomes aware that the other party will not fulfill the obligations of the contract.

Recission is the legal removal of obligations from parties in a contract. The court determines that the parties shall be returned to the point of obligation as if the contract was never executed. Essentially the contract is treated as if it never existed.

Termination is the ending of a contract before all obligations are met to fully execute the contract. There are two ways in which a contract may be terminated:

- Termination for cause: Used when a material breach of contract occurs
- Termination for convenience: Right to terminate as identified in the contract

5. Liquidated, punitive, or compensatory damages

Liquidated damages may be included in a contract to cover losses by one party which do not have a direct monetary correlation. If the other party becomes in breach of contract, they may be liable to pay an agreed upon sum for a stipulated duration. For example, if a contractor does not finish a job in time, they may be held liable for a daily penalty for every day they do not finish the work as specified in the contract.

Punitive damages are legal payments that are imposed on a defendant found guilty. These damages are in addition to compensatory damages. They should be viewed as a punishment to defendants whose conduct is considered grossly negligent or intentional.

Compensatory damages are a monetary sum awarded to a plaintiff to compensate for damages, injury, or another incurred loss. The loss by the plaintiff is a result of negligence or unlawful conduct of another party. Compensatory damages are awarded in a civil court case.

6. Statute of Frauds

The **statute of frauds** is a state law that mandates that for a contract to be enforceable must be in writing and be signed by the person against whom enforcement of the contract will be sought. This applies to most purchases of real estate transactions. Therefore, a handshake or oral agreement is not sufficient to hold a party to a transaction. Additionally, this applies to leases in which the term of the lease is greater than one year. The agreement of the term must be in writing to be enforceable.

7. Time is of the essence

Time is of the essence is a legal phrase that when used in a contract enforces parties to act in a reasonable or specified timeframe. If they fail to meet the time requirements, they may be in breach of the contract.

D. Sales contract

1. Offer and counteroffer

An offer may be made to a property owner willing to sell for less than the asking price. Once an offer is received, a counteroffer may be made. This is an offer in response to the original offer and does indicate that the original offer was rejected. There are three options upon receipt of a counteroffer: accept it, reject it, or make another offer and continue negotiations. Parties are not obligated by a contract until one accepts the other's offer. Closing costs covered by the seller may be negotiated as a part of an offer but are limited based on the down payment and loan type.

For conventional loans, seller concessions are limited by:

- Primary residence or second home:
  - Less than 10% down: 3% Maximum
  - 10%-25% down: 6% Maximum
  - 25% or more: 9% Maximum
- Investment property:
  - 2% Maximum regardless of down payment

2. Earnest money and liquidated damages

Earnest money is a deposit made from a buyer to a seller as an act of good faith to follow through on the purchase of the home. Earnest money is typically provided once an offer is accepted and typically ranges from 1% to 10% of the sales price. When the offer is accepted both parties enter into a contract. The contract doesn't require the buyer to follow through on the purchase of the home but does ensure the seller takes the house off the market while it's inspected and appraised for the buyer to obtain the necessary information to agree to the purchase. The buyer can reclaim the earnest money deposit for just cause. For example, this would apply if the home doesn't appraise for the sales price or the inspection reveals a serious defect. Earnest money is not refundable in situations where the buyer decides not to go through with the home purchase for contingencies not listed in the contract or if the buyer fails to meet the timeline outlined in the contract. If the buyer chooses to simply not go through with the purchase for no clear reason, they will forfeit the earnest money. The earnest money deposit is applied to the down payment if the contract is executed.

3. Equitable title

Equitable title refers to a person's right to obtain full ownership of a property or property interest. This indicates that the individual has full financial rights to the property.

4. Contingencies

A contingency clause in a real estate contract defines a condition or action that must be met for the contract to become binding. Some of the most common contingency clauses include:

Appraisal Contingency: Identifies a minimum value in which the property must appraise for to move forward with the purchase. If the property does not appraise for at least the specified amount the contract can be terminated and earnest money returned.

Financing Contingency: Allows the buyer to look for and obtain proper financing to complete the purchase of a property. If they are unable to, the contract can be terminated and earnest money returned.

Home Sale Contingency: Provides a buyer or seller to complete a transaction with their previous or next home before completion of the subject transaction. This allows individuals to avoid unfavorable situations such as owning two homes at once or not having one for a period of time.

Inspection Contingency: Allows the buyer the ability to inspect the home and to decide to back out of the contract if there is a significant concern due to information provided from the inspection. A cost-of-repair contingency is sometimes included in addition to the inspection contingency. This specifies a maximum dollar amount for necessary repairs resulting from the inspection. This is often based on a certain percentage of the sales price, such as 1% or 2%.

Kick-Out Clause: Allows the seller to continue to market the property. If another qualified buyer steps up, the seller gives the current buyer a specified amount of time to match the qualifications of the new buyer. Otherwise, the seller can back out of the contract and sell to the new buyer.

5. Disputes and breach of contract

If a breach of contract occurs but one party does not agree with the determination, a contract dispute takes place. This is when one party is in disagreement with the terms contained within the contract. An individual may seek legal review of the dispute to reverse any financial loss or damages. Some of the common types of disputes are as follows:

- Closing costs
- Loan fraud
- Good faith estimates
- Inspection issues
- Financing

6. Option contract and installment sales contract

An options contract is an agreement between two parties to facilitate a potential transaction involving an asset at a preset price and date. In real estate, an option contract can allow a buyer to get the exclusive right to buy the property but is not obligated to do so upon the time the option is available. The buyer pays for this right despite the fact that they may not ultimately make the purchase but it restricts the seller from entering into an agreement with anyone else until the option is decided.

An **installment sales contract** is an agreement where a buyer of real estate agrees to pay the seller the full amount of the purchase price broken up in installments over time. The buyer still takes immediate possession of the property. As leverage, the seller remains in possession of the legal title until the buyer pays in full. This is often attractive to a buyer if they are not eligible for traditional loan products for poor qualifications while also potentially avoiding fees imposed by lenders or banks. These are typically only used in specific situations where the seller has a specific purpose to sell to a particular buyer. Additionally, the seller may be able to reduce capital gains taxes by spreading out the gain over a period of time.

E. Types of agency and licensee-client relationships

An agent is defined as someone who represents a client, also referred to as a principal, to third parties in their best interest. Agency is the agreement of representation between the agent and the client. The following are types of agency:

- **General Agent**: Representation of the client for a range of activities under a specific purpose.
- **Special Agent:** The representation of an individual for a specific singular task or transaction.
- **Universal Agent**: Representation of the client in any and all matters related to their expertise.

F. Creation and termination of agency

For agency to occur, there needs to be an established purpose for the transaction and both parties must have the capacity to make the decision of their free will. Agency can be created in one of the following ways:

- **Expressed**: A written or oral agreement to representation.
- **Implied**: Actions taken that a reasonable person can assume agency has begun.
- **Necessity**: Agency without action or consent but is necessary due to extenuating circumstances.

The termination of agency may occur either voluntarily or involuntarily by either party. A voluntary termination can be done by either party, mutually, or if there is an abandonment of duties. Involuntary termination can occur in a number of ways including:

- Unlawful practices
- Failure to make payment
- Removal of licensure
- Incapacity or either party
- Expiration of agreed terms

G. Licensee obligations to parties of a transaction

Once agency is created with a client, the agent is held to certain legal responsibilities during representation of the client. These include:

- **Care and diligence**: The agent is required to meet a minimum standard of care when representing the client so that affairs are handled to satisfaction. This includes the use of skills and expertise that the agent is assumed to possess to work for the client.
- **Loyalty:** The agent shall act exclusively in the best interest of the client at all times and not pursue any activities for personal gain or that harms the client without their prior knowledge.
- **Accounting:** The agent shall properly handle and advise the client on all matters related to money or documents.
- **Obedience:** The agent shall promptly and completely follow any instructions from the client as long as they are lawful in nature.

- **Disclosure:** Any and all information related to the transaction of the client must be disclosed in a proper and timely manner.
- **Confidentiality:** The agent shall keep all information confidential even extending beyond the timeframe of any transaction.

V. REAL ESTATE PRACTICE (14)

A. Responsibilities of broker

1. Practicing within scope of expertise

A real estate broker's responsibilities are to negotiate and arrange real estate transactions. Specifically, these duties that include writing contracts, overseeing transactions, advising clients either buyers or sellers and many others. Additionally, a broker has a higher-level license than a real estate agent and can hire agents to work as a team under their supervision. A broker that has agents working under them is also called a supervising or managing broker. Supervisory responsibilities include:

- Verifies eligibility and continued licensing of all brokerage agents
- Instructs and trains agents
- Assumes responsibility for agent behavior, performance, and legal compliance
- Marketing for agents

2. Unauthorized practice of law

Real estate brokers and salespersons should maintain duties only within their scope and expertise. They are not authorized to practice law by any means. Some activities that an agent should avoid includes:

- Speculate on potential legal outcomes of a dispute
- Legal advice
- File a lawsuit
- Make arguments in court
- Draft legal paperwork

Individuals who are found to perform unauthorized legal tasks may face penalties including:

- Loss of license
- Fines
- Lawsuits
- Forfeiture of commissions

B. Brokerage agreements between the broker and principal (seller, buyer, landlord, or tenant)

1. Seller representation – Types of listing agreements

a. Exclusive right-to-sell and exclusive agency listing

An **exclusive right to sell** listing is an agreement between a seller and a real estate broker or agent to give exclusive rights to sell and market the seller's home. The seller can't hire another broker or agent for the duration of the agreement. The agreement requires the seller to provide a commission to the brokerage regardless of the agent used at closing.

An **exclusive agency listing** similarly is an agreement between a seller and brokerage for exclusive rights for the sale of a home. However, in this type of agreement, the seller retains the right to market and sell the home to a buyer without having to pay a commission.

b. Non-exclusive or open listing

An **open listing** allows the owner to place listings with multiple real estate brokers. Additionally, the homeowner retains the right to sell the home independently and avoid paying any commission to an agent. This listing type is not included in MLS.

c. Net listing (conflict of interest)

Net listings are an agreement with a seller where a real estate agent is paid by keeping the difference between what the homeowner wants to sell the home for and the actual sales price. This shifts a large amount of risk to the agent for assuming they can do better than the asking price.

d. Multiple listing service (MLS)

A multiple listing service (MLS) is a private database created, maintained and paid for by real estate professionals to help their clients buy and sell property. They can list the homes their clients have for sale and see what is available for buyers. Home sellers can't post their home directly to the MLS, because access to this database is limited to licensed agents and brokers who pay for membership. Each regional MLS has its own listings and clients may become a member of more than one. The MLS also is an information exchange among professionals in addition to the listing of properties.

2. Buyer representation

A buyer representation agreement or buyer broker agreement is a contract detailing the duties of the agent or broker with a prospective home buyer. The agreement will outline the duties of the agent as well as the specifics of the commission to be paid. The typical elements of the agreement include:

- Exclusivity
- Compensation
- Desired property description
- Required disclosures
- Term of the representation

3. Property management agreement

Property management is an agreement with a property owner and a company to handle every aspect of the rental property. A property management agreement outlines the responsibilities of the property management company. The common tasks include:

- Tenant screening
- Lease agreement drafting
- Rent collection
- Help with eviction and legal services
- Accounting
- Routine inspections
- Move-in and move out reports
- Handle tenant complaints
- Pay contractors
- Arrange repairs and maintenance
- Property showings
- Marketing

a. Accounting for funds

The accounting of property management activities is vital to the financial success of the ownership. The accounting should keep diligent records of all credits, debits, and expenses. Additionally, an awareness of tax law can be critical to the bottom line considering the large amount of available deductions. Some of the main elements of proper accounting include:

- Debits and credits
- Account balances
- Accounts payable
- Accounts receivable
- Depreciation
- Expenses
- Deductions
- Tax credits

b. Property maintenance

While property management companies are responsible for facilitating maintenance requests, they most often do not perform the maintenance themselves. They will hire licensed contractors to perform repairs necessary. These may include:

- Landscaping
- Plumbing
- HVAC
- Electrical work
- Damage repair

c. Leasing property

A lease is a contractual agreement between an owner and a renter where one party agrees to rent property owned by another party. The lease guarantees the use of an asset in exchange for regular payments for a specified period.

d. Collecting rents and security deposits

A security deposit is money provided by a renter to an owner in case of damage done to a property. Security deposits are refunded upon completion of the lease if the property was left in good condition. Security deposits typically must be paid prior to moving in and are held by the owner in an escrow account. Any interest that accrues shall be returned to the renter. The most common amount for a security deposit is equal to one month's rent but may be higher if there is reason to do so such as the presence of pets. A security deposit may also be used as replacement for rent that is not paid.

4. Termination of agreements

An agreement may be terminated either by mutually or unilaterally. If the agreement to terminate is mutual, both parties may be relieved of the contractual obligation and continue on to other endeavors. If there is no agreement, the contract may be terminated due to a breach of contract such as the agent is not honoring contractual duties or exercising an opt-out clause that is included in the contract. These may include the ability to choose a different agent within the same company or a minimum amount of time for an agent to address any grievances.

5. Services, fees, and compensation

Brokers charge brokerage fees for the work to negotiate and arrange real estate transactions. A brokerage fee is typically a flat fee or a standard percentage charged to the buyer, the seller, or both. The associated fees are typically between 1% and 2% of the loan amount. The services include:

For sellers:

- Listing homes for sale on MLS
- Advising the home seller in preparing their home for listing and showings
- Reporting information to sellers
- Submitting any offers to the seller for consideration
- Helping the seller negotiate offers to try and execute a purchase contract with a buyer
- Delivering and explain documents, disclosures, and transaction items
- Working with the seller through the closing

For buyers:

- Helping buyers locate all properties fitting their criteria
- Setting up property viewings
- Helping with offers and counteroffers
- Coordinating negotiations
- Delivering and explaining documents in the transaction process
- Coordinating inspections, reports, and repair negotiations
- Assisting buyers through to closing

C. Fair Housing

1. Equal opportunity in housing

Discrimination in lending shall not be tolerated. Applicants must have an equal opportunity to receive loans and to be treated fairly. Discrimination is prohibited as a part of:

- Fair Housing Act
- Civil Rights Act
- Home Mortgage Disclosure Act
- The Community Reinvestment Act

All applicants must receive the same level of treatment in a fair and just manner. Examples of unfair treatment include:

- Refusing to provide a loan
- Refusing to provide loan information
- Appraisal discrimination
- Imposing different terms or conditions on different people

2. Protected classes

The Equal Credit Opportunity Act prohibits discrimination in all aspects of the mortgage process on the basis of all of the following:

- Gender
- Race
- Color
- Religion
- Nationality
- Marital status
- Age
- Public assistance programs
- Exercising of rights under the Consumer Credit Protection Act

There is information that is acceptable to be questioned under the act. These include:

- Immigration status
- Permanent residency
- Credit history
- May ask if a client is receiving child support or alimony

3. Fair housing laws

The Fair Housing Act protects people from discrimination for any home-buying-related activities. The following are prohibitions for the protection of consumers:

It is illegal discrimination to take any of the following actions because of race, color, religion, sex, disability, familial status, or national origin for the sale of a property:

- Refusal to rent, sell, negotiate or make housing available
- Set different terms, conditions or privileges
- Provide a person with different housing services or facilities
- Falsely deny that housing is available for inspection, sale or rental
- Advertising must not indicate preference of any kind
- Impose different sales prices or rental charges
- Use of different qualification criteria
- Eviction
- Harassment
- Fail to complete or delay maintenance or repairs
- Assign a person to a particular building or neighborhood or section of a building or neighborhood

- Persuade, or try to persuade, homeowners to sell their homes by suggesting that people of a particular protected characteristic are about to move into the neighborhood. This is referred to as blockbusting
- Deny membership to any related organizations

Similarly, the following is prohibited from discrimination in lending practices:

- Refusal to provide a mortgage loan
- Refusal to provide information regarding loans
- Impose different terms or conditions on a loan
- Appraisal discrimination
- Refusal to purchase a loan

The specific exemptions to the Fair Housing Act are:

1. Rental of a room in a dwelling with no more than four independent units if the owner lives in one of the units
2. Housing operated by private organizations or clubs which restrict membership
3. Single-family purchase without a mortgage broker

4. Illegal practices, enforcement, and penalties

A real estate professional must adhere to the fair and ethical behavior when performing duties. Some of the prohibited practices include:

- Discrimination as per the Fair Housing Act.
- Steering is forcing a specific geographical area on an applicant based on race, religion, or ethnicity and it is strictly prohibited.
- Loan types must be clearly and properly designated so that the consumer is not mislead into thinking a product is available or obtainable that is not.
- Answering questions about a property that identifies a characteristic of the neighborhood based on race, marital status, or other prohibited identifiers. For example, if asked to find a home in an "Italian" neighborhood, the agent must refuse to answer.
- Providing listings that include discriminatory or specific language about certain groups of people.

If a complaint is filed for violation of the Fair Housing Laws, the case can go to trial. Penalties incurred may include:

- Compensation for actual damages

- Permanent injunctive relief
- Appropriate equitable relief
- Cost of attorney's fees
- Civil penalty to HUD to vindicate the public interest. The maximum civil penalties are $16,000, for a first violation of the Act; $37,500 if a previous violation has occurred within the preceding five-year period; and $65,000 if two or more previous violations have occurred within the preceding seven-year period

5. Prohibited advertising

The National Association of Realtors (NAR) Code of Ethics provides guidance for the professional to adhere to for proper behavior. Some of the prohibitions for advertising included in the code:

- Individuals shall not print, display or circulate any statement or advertisement with respect to selling or renting of a property that indicates any preference, limitations, or discrimination based on race, color, religion, sex, handicap, familial status, national origin, sexual orientation, or gender identity.
- The term "free" and similar terms in their advertising may be used only if they clearly disclose:
  - By whom they are being, or expect to be, paid
  - The amount of the payment or anticipated payment
  - Any conditions associated with the payment, offered product or service, and
- Any party interested in receiving or otherwise benefiting from an offer will have clear, thorough, advanced understanding of all the terms and conditions of the offer
- Professionals shall not offer for sale/lease or advertise a property without authority.

For mortgage products, it is prohibited to provide advertising which includes misrepresentations, expressly or by implication, in any commercial communication regarding any term of any mortgage. Regulation N prohibits misrepresentations or misleading claims in advertising for mortgages. As per section 1014.3, this includes among others:

- Type and amount of mortgage fees
- Terms, payments, or amount of loan
- Taxes or insurance associated with a loan
- Type of mortgage
- Interest rate details
- Misrepresentations of the source of commercial communication
- Ability of a consumer to be approved for a loan

When an attractive product is presented to get a potential customer engaged but then is sold a different product, this is a bait and switch. This is a prohibited practice and any advertised product must be actually available to the consumer.

It is required that advertisements are reviewed for compliance before publication. They should be reviewed to ensure they are truthful and clearly state the ability for terms and conditions to change. Products advertised must be actually available to the consumer. Negligence is not an excuse for unlawful advertising.

It is prohibited to provide advertising which includes misrepresentations, expressly or by implication, in any commercial communication regarding any term of any mortgage.

6. Housing and Urban Development (HUD)

The Department of Housing and Urban Development (HUD) oversees federal programs that address issues for Americans seeking housing. HUD's goals are to increase homeownership, support community development and increase access to affordable housing free from discrimination. The agency enforces federal housing laws, operates mortgage-supportive initiatives and distributes millions of dollars in federal grants. It is divided into a number of offices including:

- Federal Housing Administration (FHA)
- Office of Public and Indian Housing
- Office of Community Planning and Development
- Office of Healthy Homes and Lead Hazard Control
- Office of Federal Housing Enterprise Oversight
- Office of Policy Development and Research
- Office of Fair Housing and Equal Opportunity
- Government National Mortgage Association (GNMA)

The primary programs administered by HUD include:

- Federal Housing Administration mortgage and loan insurance
- Community Development Block Grants for economic development, job opportunities and housing rehabilitation
- Rental assistance in the form of Section 8 certificates or vouchers for low-income households
- Fair housing public education and enforcement

7. Americans with Disabilities Act (ADA)

The Americans With Disabilities Act (ADA) of 1990 makes it unlawful to discriminate against people with disabilities. Some of the stipulations related to real estate practices include:

Title I of the ADA applies to employment. Qualified persons with a disability who can perform the essential functions of the job with or without reasonable accommodation must not be discriminated against in job application procedures, hiring, firing, advancement, compensation, job training, and other terms, conditions, and privileges of employment. If a real estate sales office has 15 or more employees, they are subject to Title I.

Title III of the ADA prohibits entities that own, lease, lease to or operate a place of public accommodation from discriminating against the disabled. If a real estate broker or salesperson has a home office in which business is conducted with customers, that portion of the home must also be in compliance with the ADA. The ADA requires equal access and services to disabled individuals in the most integrated setting possible. Architectural and communication barriers are to be removed in existing facilities where such removal is readily achievable and can be carried out without much difficulty or expense. Examples of steps to take in order to remove barriers include installing ramps, rearranging tables and chairs, repositioning telephones, adding raised markers on elevator control buttons, widening doors, or installing offset hinges to widen doors.

D. Risk management

1. Supervision

Risk management is the identification, classification, and assessment of risks associated with an action or project. Risks are not necessarily a detrimental factor as they can be identified as either a threat or an opportunity. When buying or selling a home, each property comes with a unique set of inherent risks. It is beneficial for professionals involved in the transaction to use risk management strategies to better understand the value of the property. Risks that are identified as threats have a negative impact on the property. This may include items such as deterioration or undesirable characteristics. Opportunities may include underutilized lands or a pool that needs minor repairs. Once risks have been identified, they can be evaluated for impact and likelihood of occurrence. For example, a property may have an older furnace which would have a significant impact on the functionality of the property if it failed and due to its age, it is likely to fail sometime soon. This information helps the buyer and seller better understand the specifics of the property.

After the specific risks are identified, a mitigation strategy shall be assigned to each risk. These strategies include:

- **Avoidance**: The parties involved can choose not to take part in an action in which the risk is involved.

- **Risk reduction**: Taking action to mitigate the risk.
- **Transference:** Sharing or transferring the risk to another party.
- **Acceptance:** Moving forward with the action despite the risks presented.

2. Compliance with federal regulations; including Privacy and Do Not Contact

Non-public information can be classified as any personally identifiable information provided by a consumer to a financial institution in connection with obtaining a financial product or service. The Gramm-Leach-Bliley Act (GLBA) protects the distribution of such information in unacceptable ways.

The GLBA provides guidance to institutions regarding the sharing of non-public information. They must at a minimum disclose:

- What information is collected about its customers
- With whom the financial institution shares the information
- How the information is protected
- Opt-out options

The GLBA protects the consumer's personal financial information and requires financial institutions to explain how they will share and protect this private information. This includes disclosure of policies to the consumer related to these processes. The GLBA contains three main provisions:

- Privacy rule
- Safeguard rule
- Pre-texting rule

The Act requires a financial institution to notify the consumer if they plan to share personal information with any third parties. The consumer must be supplied with both a privacy notice and an opt-out notice. The privacy notice must contain the institution's policy on the sharing of information and the types of information shared. This must be provided no later than the time the relationship is established with the consumer. An annual notice must also be provided but it is acceptable to be posted online and not directly distributed. The privacy notice must be delivered in written form unless specifically requested with written notice to be provided electronically from the consumer. Permissible hours include 8 AM to 9 PM. Entities making calls must maintain written policies that shall be provided on demand. The person making the calls must be trained and informed of the existence of the do-not-call list. Requests from consumers to not receive calls must be internally recorded including the name and telephone number of the person.

The act provides protections to the consumer which will allow for the protection of non-public information. These include:

- Providing initial privacy notice
- Opt-out notice
- Annual privacy notice
- Prohibitions of sharing information for marketing purposes

The do-not-call registry protects consumers from unwanted solicitations on the phone. It is managed and maintained by the Federal Trade Commission (FTC). Those who choose to be on the list will limit but not eliminate any telemarketing calls from personal information. Telemarketers are required to check the list no less than once every 31 days. A consumer who is called impermissibly may file a complaint with the FTC and a penalty of up to $16,000 per incident is possible.

The do-not-call register does not eliminate all scenarios for telemarketing. There are situations where a business is exempt from the restrictions such as:

- Charities or non-profits
- A telemarketing business that has an existing relationship with a consumer may continue to call for 18 months.
- Survey calls or political polls
- Caller with written permission from a specific consumer
- An organization that makes only business-to-business calls

Consumers are able to join the list online for free by adding their telephone number to the database. They may also do so over the phone by the number provided by the FTC. Information acquired after a solicitation can be retained for 2 years.

3. Vicarious liability

Vicarious liability is a situation in which one party is held partly responsible for the unlawful actions of a third party. This does not absolve the individual from liability as well, but rather both may face legal action. This can occur in real estate related to unlawful acts during the home buying process or if a broker is responsible for the actions of an agent under their supervision.

4. Antitrust laws

The 1890 Sherman antitrust laws were enacted to ensure a fair and competitive market for real estate transactions. Some of the prohibitions included in the act includes:

Price fixing is an agreement on a standard set price across multiple companies. The rigid setting of fees would not allow for an open and fair market for customers. This applies to competing brokers, real estate governing bodies, or multiple listing organizations in regards to sale conditions, fees, or management rates.

Group boycotting is the act of two or more brokers conspiring against another business or coming together to agree to withhold their patronage to reduce competition.

The allocation of markets or customers is the agreement to divide areas with customers so that there is no competition within markets.

Tie-in agreements are an agreement to sell one product but only with the condition that the buyer also purchases a different product or service.

The penalty for violation of the Sherman Antitrust Laws can be a fine of up to $100,000 and up to three years in prison for individuals. A corporation may be fined up to $1 million.

5. Fraud and misrepresentation

Fraud and misrepresentation in real estate transactions are both ways in which misinformation is provided to a client. There is an important difference between the two. Fraud is the intentional providing of information to deceive an individual into performing a desired act, such as signing a contract or entering into an agreement. Misrepresentation is the unintentional providing of incorrect information. While fraud is a more severe penalty and wrongdoing, both have consequences and can affect the viability of an established contract.

6. Types of insurance

a. Errors and Omissions

Errors and omissions insurance (E&O) is malpractice insurance coverage for real estate professionals to pay for claims related to error, omission, or negligence in an agent's duties. Not all actions are covered under E&O. Common exclusions include claims resulting from dishonest or criminal acts, if the agent caused bodily harm or death to another person, or if there is damage to someone's property. Often brokers may include coverage as a part of employment.

b. General Liability

General liability insurance covers claims resulting from bodily injury or property damage. Additionally, the insurance will cover medical expenses and attorney fees related to these claims.

VI. PROPERTY DISCLOSURES AND ENVIRONMENTAL ISSUES (8)

A. Property conditions and environmental issues

1. Hazardous substances

a. Lead-based paint

The use of lead in paint was prohibited beginning in 1978. Exposure to lead paint and specifically, inhalation or ingestion of paint flakes can cause severe medical issues. The 1992 Residential Lead-Based Paint Hazard Reduction Act required any licensed individual involved in the sale, lease, management, construction, or appraisal of a property built before 1978 to provide clear notification to parties involved in the transaction.

b. Asbestos, radon, and mold

In 1978, asbestos, a construction material used commonly than in many parts of the home, was banned. Therefore, any home transaction involving a property that was built before 1978 may include this hazardous material. Asbestos is linked to health complications due to its ability to become friable, which means it will break down into particles small enough to be inhaled. Asbestos has been linked to respiratory diseases such as lung cancer. Due to the friability, asbestos is not easy to remove since the disturbances causes the particles to become airborne. A different mitigation strategy that may be acceptable is encapsulation. This is when the material identified with asbestos is enclosed with some other material.

Radon is an odorless, colorless radioactive gas that is produced by the natural decay of radioactive substances. It is a concern in the ground below a property in which case it can seep through the foundation and enter the home. Radon also has been linked to respiratory issues including lung cancer due to inhalation over time. Radon tests can be performed and if they are determined to be above the acceptable limit, mitigation must be implemented. The acceptable limit is determined on the state level but the generally accepted action level established by the World Health Organization is 2.7 pCi/L. Radon mitigation systems will extract the airborne gas and reduce levels.

Mold is organic growth in areas of high moisture. Mold is common in areas of the home such as around leaks in roofs, windows, or pipes, or where there has been flooding. Exposure to mold can be dangerous due to the effect on the air quality in the home. Some individuals may have a minor allergic reaction but others such as black mold can cause a serious threat to health including respiratory issues.

c. Groundwater contamination and underground storage tanks

Groundwater contamination occurs from the seeping of substances such as gasoline, oil, road salts and chemicals into the groundwater. This causes it to become unsafe and unfit for human use and can cause serious health effects if ingested. The presence or potential presence of groundwater contamination can trigger the need for an environmental site assessment.

By EPA definition, an underground storage tank (UST) is defined as "a tank and any underground piping connected to the tank that has at least 10 percent of its combined volume underground." UST's may contain petroleum or other certain hazardous substances, such as methane and solvents. If a property contains an underground storage tank, it must be inspected for leaking. UST's that are failing can contaminate the groundwater, leading to hazardous drinking water conditions. It is common for homes built before the late 1970s to include UST's. An owner of a UST that is regulated by the federal government must meet the following requirements:

- Meet all leak detection requirements
- Meet overfill, spill, and corrosion protection requirements
- Be registered with the appropriate regulatory authorities
- Perform site checks and take corrective action in response to spills, leaks, and overfills
- Follow regulatory guidelines during the installation of new tanks and closure of any existing tanks
- Have routine checks performed for corrosion and leak detection systems
- Maintain records

d. Waste disposal sites and brownfields

A brownfield is a property that includes the presence or potential presence of a hazardous substance, pollutant, or contaminant. This factor makes construction, renovation, or reuse of the property difficult. According to the EPA, it is estimated that there are more than 450,000 brownfields in the U.S. The EPA's Land Use and Revitalization program has been instituted to help clean up these properties to realize benefits such as an increase in local tax bases, job growth, and environmental improvements. The program provides grants to help mitigate the higher costs of environmental complications. These grants support the revitalization efforts by funding environmental assessment, cleanup, and job training activities.

e. Flood plains, flood zones, and flood insurance

Flood plains are lands bordering rivers and streams that normally are dry but are covered with water during floods. Properties on flood plains are at high risk of damage due to flooding.

Flood zones are geographic areas that FEMA has classified according to varying levels of flood risk. These zones are depicted on a community's Flood Insurance Rate Map (FIRM). The zone a property falls in determines the requirement for flood insurance. Those in high-risk areas are required to have flood insurance. Those in the moderate risk levels are not required but should consider the purchase of flood insurance. The general zones are as follows:

High-Risk Zones:

- Zone A: Areas with a 1% annual chance of flooding and a 26% chance of flooding over the life of a 30-year mortgage.
- Zone V: Coastal areas with a 1% or greater chance of flooding and an additional hazard associated with storm waves. These areas have a 26% chance of flooding over the life of a 30-year mortgage.

Moderate or Less Risk Zones:

- Zone B: Area of moderate flood hazard, usually the area between the limits of the 100-year and 500-year floods.
- Zone D: Areas with possible but undetermined flood hazards.

2. Clean Air and Water Acts

The Clean Air Act of 1970 regulates air emissions from stationary and mobile sources. The law authorizes the Environmental Protection Agency (EPA) to establish National Ambient Air Quality Standards (NAAQS) to protect public health and public welfare and to regulate emissions of hazardous air pollutants. The purpose of the act is to regulate air pollutant emissions and determines acceptable levels for emissions.

The Clean Water Act (CWA) regulates discharges of pollutants into the waters of the United States and establishes quality standards for surface waters. The act includes the EPA implemented pollution control programs such as wastewater standards and national water quality criteria recommendations for pollutants in surface waters. The CWA made it unlawful to discharge any pollutant from a point source into navigable waters, unless a permit was obtained.

3. Environmental Protection Agency (EPA)

a. Comprehensive Environmental Response, Compensation, and Liability Act (CERCLA)

The Comprehensive Environmental Response, Compensation, and Liability Act (CERCLA or Superfund) provides Federal funds to clean up uncontrolled or abandoned hazardous-waste sites due to accidents, spills, and other emergency releases of pollutants and contaminants into the environment. EPA also is tasked with identifying parties responsible for any release and assure their cooperation in the cleanup. When responsible parties cannot be identified or do not cooperate, the Act gives EPA the funds and means necessary to implement a cleanup process for the contaminated site.

b. Superfund Amendment and Reauthorization Act (SARA)

The Superfund Amendments and Reauthorization Act amended the Comprehensive Environmental Response, Compensation, and Liability Act. The changes to the Act include:

- Stressed the importance of permanent remedies and innovative treatment technologies in cleaning up hazardous waste sites
- Required Superfund actions to consider the standards and requirements found in other State and Federal environmental laws and regulations
- Provided new enforcement authorities and settlement tools
- Increased State involvement
- Increased the focus on human health problems posed by hazardous waste sites
- Encouraged greater citizen participation in making decisions on how sites should be cleaned up
- Increased the size of the trust fund to $8.5 billion.
- Revised the Hazard Ranking System

c. Environmental site assessments (including Phase I and II studies) and impact statements

An Environmental Site Assessment (ESA) is a process of evaluating the environmental liability of a real estate asset. The process includes the conducting of "all appropriate inquiry" into the past or present uses of a property to determine whether the property is impacted by a recognized environmental condition (REC). The ESA process includes a site inspection, a review of historical records of the property, and research of records available at government agencies. Once this information is gathered and evaluated, an Environmental Site Assessment Report is completed which includes an opinion on any identified release of hazardous substances at the property.

A site assessment can be Phase I, Phase II or Phase III. A Phase I primarily assesses the likelihood that a site is contaminated through visual observations, historical use reviews, and regulatory records. A Phase II assesses whether contamination is in fact present. Phase III is used when contamination has already been identified. The tasks associated with each phase are typically as follows:

Phase I Environmental Site Assessment:

- Review of records
- Visual inspection of the property's current condition
- Visual inspection of adjoining properties

- Interviews with current property owners, operators, occupants, and local government officials
- Goal is to assess the likelihood that the property has been contaminated

Phase II Environmental Site Assessment:

- Soil and water sampling
- Inspection of interior spaces for hazardous substances such as mold, radon, or lead paint
- Identification of wetlands, ecological resources, or endangered species that may prevent certain land uses
- Goal is to assess actual presence of environmental contaminants

Phase III Site Assessment:

- Only used when contamination has been identified
- Determines the extent of the contamination
- Begins the development of a remediation plan
- Estimation of the cost for remediation

If the assessment determines that any action is needed that will affect the environment, an environmental impact statement (EIS) is required. An EIS is a document prepared to describe the effects of proposed activities on the environment. The elements of the EIS must include:

- Description of the proposed project
- Explain why the project is being considered
- Identify alternatives
- Detail the environmental consequences

d. Wetlands protection

Wetlands are areas of land where water covers the soil or is present at or near the surface of the soil all year or for varying periods of time during the year. The water creates favorable conditions for the growth of special plants and promotes the development of wetland soils. Wetlands are divided into two general categories: coastal or tidal wetlands and inland or non-tidal wetlands. The Federal Government protects wetlands through regulation, acquisition, or through incentives and disincentives. Wetlands shall not be built on without difficult to obtain permits and need to be identified as a part of any real estate transactions.

B. Disclosure obligations and liability

Disclosure information and obligations are set by state law but sellers are generally required to provide a written disclosure for information regarding anything they have knowledge of regarding the property's condition that may affect its value. Some of the most common required disclosures include:

- Repairs or damage to the property
- A death in the home
- Neighborhood factors affecting the desirability of the location
- Increased risk of damage from a natural disaster or other hazard
- Water damage
- HOA information
- Missing basic items that are reasonably expected to be present
- Historical designations or restrictions
- Termite damage
- Environmental risks

A lack of proper or withholding of disclosure information may result in a lawsuit or a breach of contract.

VII. FINANCING AND SETTLEMENT (7)

A. Financing concepts and components

1. Methods of financing

a. Mortgage financing – conventional and non-conventional loans

Lenders must evaluate a borrower's ability to repay to determine if they can in fact meet the requirements of the loan terms. For a loan to be considered conventional there are minimum requirements that must be met. This ensures a minimum level of credentials for the borrower that provides a reasonable expectation that the loan can be paid back. This includes:

- Limiting the debt-to-income ratio of the borrower to 36% in most cases.
- Minimum down payment of typically at least 5%
- Minimum credit score of 620

Conventional loans often require a higher minimum down payment amounts than government-backed loans such as FHA which requires 3.5% or VA which can be as low as 0%. While low down payment loans exist, lenders will not often accept less than 5% down and anything less than 20% will require Private Mortgage Insurance (PMI). The cost of the PMI will vary depending on the down payment and other factors such as credit score.

A conventional mortgage also has requirements outside of the borrower's qualifications. The loan will not have more risky aspects such as:

- Interest-only payments
- Negative Amortization
- Balloon Payments
- Loan terms longer than 30 years
- Excess points or fees

A non-conventional loan is one that does not have to follow traditional mortgage loan requirements. These loans offer more flexible qualification requirements and are often backed by government entities such as The Federal Housing Administration, the U.S. Department of Veterans Affairs, and the U.S. Department of Agriculture.

b. Seller financing – land contract/contract for deed

Seller financing involves a loan for a property directly from the seller of the home. This non-conventional loan can allow homebuyers to avoid strict mortgage requirements but may include some fewer desirable aspects such as higher interest rates. Additionally, an assumable loan allows a borrower to take on an existing loan including all aspects of that loan such as the term and interest rate. An assumption clause in a mortgage contract allows the seller to pass the responsibility of the existing mortgage onto the buyer. This may be attractive if the terms of the existing loan are more attractive than what is currently available for the buyer. This is not a common practice as banks don't often allow it on conventional mortgages. They are more common for government-backed mortgages such as FHA, VA, or USDA.

2. Lien theory vs. title theory and deed of trust

In title theory, the title is held in the lender's name until the final payment is made, when the title is passed or re-conveyed to the borrower.

In lien theory, the title to the property is held in the name of the borrower with a security interest or lien to the property being granted to the lender. If the property is sold, typically, the lien would be paid off and released. That process is taken care of by the title company.
In addition to the manner in which the title is held to the property, there are differences in the way foreclosures are handled. In title theory, where ownership of the property is held by the lender, foreclosures are a judicial process that involves an expensive lawsuit and might take months or years to resolve. In Lien Theory, the foreclosure process is non-judicial and handled by a trustee.

3. Sources of financing (primary and secondary mortgage markets, and seller financing)

The primary mortgage market is the name for the transactions involving the origination and execution of mortgage loans. These loans are then packaged and sold in the secondary mortgage market.

The secondary mortgage market is where mortgages are bought and sold as securities. An aggregator is an entity that purchases mortgages from financial institutions and then securitizes them into mortgage-backed securities (MBS).

A mortgage investor purchases loans on the secondary market from the primary market. Loans which are originated in the primary market are grouped into mortgage-backed securities (MBS) which can be purchased as an investment. Fannie Mae and Freddie Mac are the largest mortgage investors in the world who buy loans that fit their underwriting guidelines.

Fannie Mae and Freddie Mac are government entities that purchase most of the home loans in the US and provide liquidity to lenders as needed. This allows lenders to be able to have the assets necessary to provide a larger and wide-ranging number of loans. This is done by Fannie Mae and Freddie Mac packaging loans into attractive mortgage-backed securities in which payment is more dependable. This helps to stabilize the market and lower interest rates based on the reduced risk. The sister company, Ginnie Mae, is the entity responsible for payments of mortgage bonds and does not fall under Fannie Mae and Freddie Mac's responsibilities.

4. Types of loans and loan programs

There are a number of different loan types that may be used to fit an individual's specific scenarios. Some of the more common loan types include:

Fixed-rate mortgages include an interest rate that will not change over the full life of the loan. Because of this, there is a constant payment for the principal and interest for the full amortization schedule of the loan. The total home payment can change due to variances in the property taxes, insurance, or PMI.

An adjustable-rate loan has a rate that may fluctuate throughout the life or a portion of the loan term. The rate for the adjustable period is determined by the fully indexed rate which is the margin plus the index. ARM's have caps that the rate cannot exceed regardless of the index and margin. The lifetime cap limits the increase over the life of the loan and the periodic cap limits the increase from one period to the next.

Balloon loans include a lump sum payment portion of the principal balance instead of fully amortizing with payments over the life of the loan. Consumers will pay a portion of the loan or an interest-only period which have lower payments. Then at the end, there is a remaining balance that must be paid. Balloon loans are considered high-risk options.

A reverse mortgage provides payment from a lender to a borrower that taps into the existing equity of a home. The equity is reduced as the payments are made. The lender is not buying the home however and the borrower is indeed still responsible for the increase in debt that results from the payments. This is often settled by the selling of the home at the completion of the loan.

The Home Equity Line of Credit (HELOC) is a way for a borrower to tap into the equity of an existing home loan for other purposes. HELOC's and home equity loans are, but there are some differences. One of which is that the home equity loan typically will have a fixed rate while the HELOC will be an adjustable-rate with interest calculated per diem. The line of credit can be accessed up to the maximum amount agreed upon by the borrower and lender. The borrower can use as much or as little as they wish. HELOCs often have a draw period in which there are interest-only payments and then a repayment period where the payment includes both interest and principal.

There are two types of loans for construction:

Construction-to-permanent loans is a single loan comprised of two parts. Therefore, there is only one closing and terms can be set on the mortgage after construction such as a maximum rate. The payments made during construction are interest only.

A construction-only loan is actually two separate loans: one solely for the construction of the home and then a mortgage. Because of this the fees for the loans are separate and require two sets

Interest-only mortgages as the name suggests, include payments that consist only of paying interest. This means that there is no pay down of the principal balance as the loan progresses. These mortgages will have a set period of interest only and then begin a phase of increased payments that include a portion for paying down the principal.

5. Mortgage clauses

A clause is simply a particular section of a contract. Some types of clauses that are common in real estate transactions may include:

Acceleration clause: Requires the entire amount of the debt to be due immediately. An acceleration clause may activate when the borrower misses a specified number of payments.

Subordination clause: Outlines the hierarchy of liens on a property. Loans must have an order in which they are to be paid off. This clause establishes where available funds will go first. This is often useful in a foreclosure scenario where a borrower has failed to make payments and a determination must be made as to where available funds are to be allocated.

Prepayment penalty clause: A penalty will be charged to the borrower if the loan is paid off early. This would occur if additional principal payments are made by the borrower to reduce the balance and thus the loan term. This reduces the amount of interest paid over the life of the loan.

Alienation or due-on-sale clause: Requires a borrower to pay the entire loan balance if the property is being sold. This is common to prevent a buyer of a property from assuming the current loan which may include more favorable or outdated terms.

Release clause: Allows an individual property in a blanket mortgage to be released from any liens by the lender. This is common when an individual has multiple properties and wishes to combine them under a single loan.

B. Lender Requirements

1. FHA requirements

FHA loans are government-backed loans. Therefore, an FHA loan has a low minimum down payment of 3.5% but the credit score of the individual must be at least 580. If the credit score falls between 500 and 580 the minimum down payment increases to 10%. FHA has maximum debt ratios which are 31% on the front end and 43% on the back end. The loans actually come from an FHA approved lender and not FHA itself. The backing of the loan comes from the required upfront mortgage insurance premium cost that is included as a part of the closing costs. This does not relieve the borrower however of the annual PMI requirement. In addition to traditional mortgages, FHA also offers the following:

- Home equity conversion loans
- 203k home improvement loans
- Energy-efficient mortgage program
- Graduated payment loans

The determination of the interest rate for FHA mortgages is determined by a number of factors similar to conventional loans including:

- Credit score
- Amount of loan
- Down payment
- Type of rate
- Discount points

The FHA establishes minimum property standards that may cause properties acceptable under conventional loans, to not be eligible for FHA financing. The standard is established to protect both the lender and the borrower from entering into an agreement with a sub-standard property that may require extensive repairs or limit the ability of a resale.

The minimum standards can be divided into three categories:

- Safety: Any aspects of the property which may be considered a risk to the safety of the occupant or any visiting individuals must be addressed. This may include certain areas of the home which are not up to code such as railing heights or tripping hazards
- Security: The home should adequately protect the occupant and possessions inside
- Soundness: The property may not have aspects that may compromise the structural integrity of the home. This may include rotting of structural supports or excessive foundation cracking

FHA will assess the severity of the defect and does not require the repair of anything determined to be minor or cosmetic

FHA sets limits on the amount that can be borrowed. It is dependent on the geographical area in which the loan is taken and the median sale price in that area. However, it can never be higher than the ceiling or lower than the floor in any area. Single-family forward loan limits are 115% of median house prices, subject to the floor and ceiling on the limits. Any areas where the loan limit exceeds this floor is considered a high-cost area, and FHA is required to set its maximum loan limit ceiling for high-cost areas at 150% of the national conforming limit.

2. VA requirements

VA loans are available for veterans to receive more beneficial loans. The loans are issued by private lenders but backed by the US Department of Veteran affairs. Some of the benefits of the VA loans include:

- 0% down payment
- No PMI
- Lower interest rates
- Easier to qualify

VA entitlement is a benefit to veterans seeking a first-time mortgage. It refers to the amount of money that is guaranteed to lenders in the event of default. While VA loans can require 0% down, there is a limit based on the entitlement. There are two scenarios to determine the amount:

- $36,000 for loans less than $144,000
- 25% of loans greater than $144,000

A Certificate of Eligibility (COE) verifies to the lender that the applicant is eligible for a VA loan. To obtain the certificate, the borrower must provide evidence of service depending on their status:

- For Veterans/Current or former National Guard/Reserve members who have been activated for Federal active service
  - DD Form 214
- Active Duty Servicemember
  - A current statement of service
- Current National Guard or Reserve member not Federal active service
  - Statement of Service

A funding fee of 2.15% for VA loans is required by all but certain exempt veterans. A down payment of 5 percent or more will reduce the fee to 1.5% and a 10 percent down payment will reduce it to 1.25%.

All Reserve or National Guard must pay 2.40%. A down payment of 5 percent or more will reduce the fee to 1.75% and a 10 percent down payment will reduce it to 1.5%.

The following are exemptions to paying the funding fee:

- Veterans receiving VA compensation for service-connected disabilities.
- Veterans who would be entitled to receive compensation for service-connected disabilities if they did not receive retirement pay.
- Surviving spouses of veterans who died in service or from service-connected disabilities

The funding fee is eligible to be financed as a part of the loan.

3. Buyer qualification and Loan to Value (LTV)

Underwriting is the evaluation of a borrower to determine their suitability for a loan. They will evaluate the applicant for their ability-to-repay and determine if the lender shall proceed with issuing the loan. The ability to repay rule is mostly centered around 8 factors:

- Current or expected income
- Employment status
- Mortgage payment
- Any additional loans secured by the same property
- Property taxes, insurance, and any other associated costs related to the property
- Monthly debts
- Debt-to-income ratios
- Credit history

The debt-to-income ratio is a representation of the amount of monthly debts and obligations a borrower will have compared to the monthly income. This is a common way for the lender to assess the borrower's ability to repay. There are two types of debt ratios. The front end or housing ratio is the total mortgage payment only divided by the monthly income. The back-end ratio is the Mortgage payment and all other debt payments divided by the income:

$$Front\ End\ DTI = \frac{(Mortgage)}{Monthly\ Income}$$

$$Back\ End\ DTI = \frac{(Mortgage + Debt\ Payments)}{Monthly\ Income}$$

The income must be calculated by taking the yearly income and dividing it by 12. The Mortgage payment includes all principal, interest, property tax, insurance, and PMI. Other debt obligations are those which require a monthly minimum payment such as student loans or credit cards. This does not include all monthly expenses such as utility bills or grocery costs.

The housing-to-income ratio also known as the front-end ratio is an evaluation of income relative to only the proposed total mortgage payment. This includes principal, interest, taxes, hazard insurance, and PMI if applicable. Often the desirable front-end is 28%.

The total debt ratio is also referred to as the back-end ratio. This is the ratio of all proposed monthly obligations including the total mortgage payment and any others to the monthly income. This may include loans, credit cards, or other debts. A favorable back-end ratio is typically considered to be 36% but can be as high as 50% in some circumstances.

Not all assets are considered similar in their ability to be used for loans. The most common types of assets which are allowed includes:

- Earnest money deposit
- Checking or savings account
- Business accounts
- Stocks
- Bonds
- Mutual funds
- 401k or other retirement funds (to a certain percentage)
- Acceptable gifts
- Sale of assets
- Verified deposits

Some assets which are not acceptable include:

- Cash on hand
- Sweat equity (except in certain circumstances)
- Lender contributions
- Unvested funds
- Undocumented funds
- Illegally obtained funds

Loan-to-value ratio is simply the amount financed divided by the value of the home as determined either by the sale price for a purchase transaction or the appraised value for a refinance:

$$LTV = \frac{Amount\ of\ Loan}{Value\ of\ Property}$$

The maximum LTV is determined by the minimum amount of money a borrower must put down to qualify for the loan. This is determined by the type of loan whether it be conventional, FHA, VA, etc. The loan-to-value ratio is also the factor used to determine the need and extent of private mortgage insurance (PMI).

4. Hazard and flood insurance

The hazard insurance must show that it fully covers damage from natural occurrences. This may include an endorsement or separate policy from the original. The claims must be settled however on a replacement cost basis and not actual value. Hazard insurance is typically paid for through an escrow account along with property taxes and PMI as applicable.

Flood insurance is an additional aspect of hazard insurance for certain properties. FEMA requirements stipulate that the flood coverage must be at least the lesser of:

- The maximum amount of NFIP coverage available for the particular property type, or
- The outstanding principal balance of the loan, or
- The insurable value of the structure.

The requirement for flood insurance is determined by the location of the property and whether or not they are in the specific designated flood zones. The Flood Emergency Management Agency (FEMA) provides flood zone maps. Flood insurance is required in high-risk areas designated as Zone A and Zone V.

The amount of flood insurance is determined by the type of property and the limits of the property. The minimum amount of flood insurance is the least of the following three:

- The National Flood Insurance Program (NFIP) Maximum
- The insurable value of the property
- The loan amount

NFIP typically cannot exceed $250,000 for the structure of the home and $100,000 for personal property

Private flood insurance can also be purchased to satisfy the requirements. The advantage is the limits on private insurance are much higher than the maximums provided by NFIP. The private flood insurance cost is a function of the FEMA hazard area. The more high-risk area, the higher the cost.

If there is no insurance on a property due to reasons such as failure to pay, the lender can force insurance on the borrower so that the property is still protected. This is known as force-placed insurance.

<u>5. Private mortgage insurance (PMI) and mortgage insurance premium (MIP)</u>

Private Mortgage Insurance (PMI) is protection for the lender. The borrower pays a monthly fee that is used to insure the lender in the event of default.

While PMI does not cover the borrower in the event of default, it helps the lender to have more confidence in the borrower's ability to repay. This has allowed less qualified borrowers to get loans, especially in the case of lower down payment amounts.

The yearly cost of PMI is typically between 0.5% to 1.0% of the total loan amount. This yearly cost is divided into equal monthly payments as a part of the borrower's monthly obligations. The amount is often a function of the down payment amount. The more put down, the less the yearly premium will be.

FHA loans will require an upfront mortgage insurance premium (UFMIP). This is required to be able to provide the borrower with a reduced down payment amount to offset the risk the lender is taking with the reduced equity. This is a one-time payment as a part of the closing costs. This does not replace the need for monthly mortgage insurance. The UFMIP will typically be about 1.75% of the total loan amount.

One of the many benefits of VA loans is they do not require PMI.

IF the initial down payment is less than 20%, PMI will end automatically at a scheduled LTV of 78%. This also holds true if extra payments are applied to the principal despite the fact that a loan may have the necessary equity to remove PMI there is a seasoning period in which the borrower must wait to apply to remove the payment. This period is a minimum of 2 years.

PMI is required if the loan to value ratio is greater than 80%. If 80% is not achieved, the PMI will automatically be stopped at an LTV of 78% in accordance with the amortization schedule. A borrower can apply to have PMI removed a minimum of 2 years after the origination of the loan if there is reason to believe the loan to value has decreased. This may be because of principal payoff or an increased appraisal.

C. Federal Financing Regulations and Regulatory Bodies

1. Truth-in-Lending and Regulation Z

Regulation Z also known as the Truth in Lending Act has the goal to provide consumers with better information about the true costs of credit and to protect them from certain misleading practices by the lending industry. Lenders must disclose interest rates, allow borrowers the right to cancel within a specified period, use clear language about loan and credit terms, and respond to complaints, among other provisions.

In addition, the act:

- Protects consumers against inaccurate and unfair credit billing and credit card practices
- Provides consumers with rescission rights
- Provides rate caps on certain dwelling-secured loans
- Imposes limitations on home equity lines of credit and certain closed-end home mortgages
- Provides minimum standards for most dwelling-secured loans
- Delineates and prohibits unfair or deceptive mortgage lending practices.

The TILA and Regulation Z do not, however, tell financial institutions how much interest they may charge or whether they must grant a consumer a loan.

TILA section 1026.24(i) provides prohibited acts in advertising. Some of the requirements include:

- Only advertising for products actually available
- Providing clear disclosures
- Requirements for mentioning of interest rates
- Triggering terms
- Disclosure requirements of rates and payments
- Disclosure requirements specifically for TV and radio
- Prohibited practices including:
    o Misleading of the term fixed rate
    o Misleading comparisons
    o Misrepresentation about government endorsements
    o Current lender's name
    o Debt elimination
    o Improper use of the term "counselor"

- o Misuse of foreign languages

Section 1026.4(b) of Regulation Z gives examples of finance charges generally applicable to consumer loans:

- Interest and any amount payable under an add-on or discount system of additional charges.
- Service, transaction, activity, and carrying charges.
- Points, loan fees, assumption fees, finder's fees, and similar charges.
- Appraisal, investigation, and credit report fees.
- Premiums or other charges for any guarantee or insurance protecting the creditor against the consumer's default or other credit loss.
- Charges imposed on a creditor by another person for purchasing or accepting a consumer's obligation.
- Premiums or other charges for credit life, accident, health, or loss-of-income insurance, written in connection with a credit transaction.
- Premiums or other charges for insurance against loss of or damage to property, or against liability arising out of the ownership or use of property.
- Discounts for the purpose of inducing payment by a means other than the use of credit.
- Charges or premiums paid for debt cancellation or debt suspension coverage

Regulation Z defines a finance charge as the cost of credit as a dollar amount. The calculation is a process that involves determining which of many fees associated with a loan's origination and closing are included in the charge. Section 1026.4(c)(7) of Regulation Z details the fees excluded from the finance charge if a transaction is secured by real property or is a residential mortgage transaction:

- Fees for title examination, abstract of title, title insurance, property survey, and similar purposes.
- Fees for preparing loan-related documents, such as deeds, mortgages, and reconveyance or settlement documents.
- Notary and credit-report fees.
- Property appraisal fees or fees for inspections to assess the value or condition of the property if the service is performed prior to closing, including fees related to pest-infestation or flood-hazard determinations.
- Amounts required to be paid into escrow or trustee accounts if the amounts would not otherwise be included in the finance charge."

2. TILA-RESPA Integrated Disclosures (TRID)

TRID was introduced to reduce the amount of paperwork involved in mortgage transactions and to provide more clarity, understanding, and accuracy for the borrower. The goal of the act was also to reduce confusion.

The integrated disclosure rule was meant to try to simplify and streamline the mortgage process for applicants. This was made in an effort to reduce confusion that was found to be common in many mortgage transactions. Some main changes of the rule include replacing the Good Faith Estimate with the loan estimate and the final HUD-1 form with the closing disclosure. TRID applies to most closed-end mortgages and does not apply to HELOCs, reverse mortgages, and a dwelling not attached to a real property.

Most closed-end loans which are secured by a property are covered by TILA with some exceptions. These exceptions include:

- Reverse mortgages
- HELOC's
- Loans secured by a home that is not attached to a property (i.e. mobile home)
- Loans made by an entity that provides 5 or fewer mortgages in a calendar year

Some common violations of the TRID include:

- Date of issuance for the Loan estimate or closing disclosure
- Failing to provide seller's CD
- Consistency in fee names
- Incorrect information such as contact

a. Consumer Financial Protection Bureau (CFPB)

The Consumer Financial Protection Bureau aims to support, educate, and protect consumers seeking and using loans. The protection extends beyond mortgages and includes car, student, and others as well. The CFPB provides tools and examples to consumers as they progress through the loan process so that they may make informed decisions.

The CFPB also protects consumers by taking action against those who participate in illegal or predatory practices. Complaints can be filed and companies are required to cooperate and respond.

The CFPB is also subject to the laws governing federal agencies to ensure they proceed in a fair and responsible manner. They have accountability to the President and Congress including annual reports, audits, and semi-annual testifying to Congress. The CFPB is also subject to veto by the Federal Stability Oversight Council (FSOC) and must consult with federal banking agencies when establishing new rules. There are a number of checks and balances towards the CFPB including a capped budget, small business rule processes, mandatory cost-benefit analyses, and mandatory stakeholder involvement and comment.

CFPB has oversight over a large number of entities to ensure enforcement of federal consumer finance laws. It has authority over banks, thrifts, and credit unions with assets over $10 Billion and any affiliates. Also, CFPB oversees non-bank mortgage originators and servicers, payday lenders, and private student lenders of any size. CFPB also maintains a list of depository institutions and affiliates.

The CFPB allows consumers to submit complaints if they believe a violation has occurred. Complaints are submitted online or over the phone. Complaints are then submitted to the company in question for a response. Complaints are published with personal information removed for the education of the public.

b. Loan Estimate (LE)

A loan estimate replaces the Good Faith Estimate (GFE). A loan estimate will be standardized with all lenders and will clearly state the terms and estimated fees. This will make shopping for a mortgage and comparing loan offers easier for consumers.

The loan estimate is the initial form received after the application is received. It must be provided within 3 business days after receipt of the application. The information provided includes a best estimate of the interest rate, monthly payment, and closing costs for the loan. Also included will be anticipated property taxes and insurance costs.

The loan estimate shall also include any features of the loan including prepayment penalties or negative amortization. The loan estimate is not an indication of approval.

The loan estimate expires 10 days after issue. Expiration of the loan estimate is considered a change in circumstance and any further progress would require a revised LE.

Estimated information included in the loan estimate includes among others:

- Interest rate
- Monthly payment
- Total closing costs
- Prepayment penalties
- Amounts that can increase after closing
- Mortgage insurance
- End of mortgage insurance
- Loan costs
- Prepaids
- Taxes
- Cash to close

c. Closing Disclosure (CD)

The HUD-1 statement has been replaced with the closing disclosure. The CD is implemented to make the costs and fees clear. The CD provides the actual costs at closing but can vary from the loan estimate within certain limitations.

Closing disclosure provides the final costs and specifications of the loan. The information provided includes:

- Final interest rate
- Monthly payment
- Closing costs
- Cash to close
- Prepayment penalty
- Costs that may increase after closing
- Breakdown of closing costs
- Total cost of the loan
- APR
- Total interest paid over the life of the loan
- Late payment penalties
- Indication of negative amortization
- Loan assumption indication

3. Real Estate Settlement Procedures Act (RESPA)

RESPA was enacted in 1974 by Congress to allow consumers the ability to obtain costs for settlement services at closing so that they may have the ability to choose appropriately between loan providers. RESPA also includes provisions to protect consumers from excessive settlement costs or lenders who participate in prohibited acts such as kickbacks or referral fees.

RESPA stands for the Real Estate Settlement Procedures Act and is overseen by the U.S. Department of Housing and Urban Development (HUD).

The main purposes of RESPA include:

- Providing certain disclosures in connection with the real estate process so home purchasers can make informed decisions regarding their real estate transactions
- To prohibit certain unlawful practices by real estate settlement providers, such as kickbacks and referral fees, that can drive up settlement costs for home buyers.

RESPA includes a number of prohibited practices for the protection of consumers. They include:

- Section 6: Right to proper servicing of the loan
- Section 8: Prohibiting a person from receiving anything of value for a referral of settlement services or being paid without performing a service.
- Section 9: Prohibits the requirement of settlement services from a particular company directly or indirectly
- Section 10: Limits the amount of money a lender may hold in escrow

a. Referrals

Section 8 of RESPA prohibits any person involved in a mortgage transaction from giving or accepting anything of value for referrals of settlement service business. It also prohibits a person from giving or accepting any part of a charge for services that are not performed. These are also known as kickbacks, fee-splitting and unearned fees. Violations of Section 8 are subject to criminal and civil penalties including a fine up to $10,000 and prison up to one year.

A lender may own or have a partial interest in real estate, mortgage, or title companies. RESPA requires that when one of these entities refers the applicant to another affiliated provider, the loan applicant receives an Affiliated Business Arrangement Disclosure. This disclosure must include the details of the relationship and the estimate for the service. It shall be provided at the time of the referral and no later.

Kickbacks are compensation paid illegally to an individual involved in a real estate transaction so that they may provide a specific recommendation, service, or decision. This would be a sales agent being paid by a third-party service to be recommended.

b. Rebates

A real estate professional can agree to rebate a portion of his/her commission to a consumer. However, some states do have laws prohibiting the payments of rebates to unlicensed individuals.

4. Equal Credit Opportunity Act (ECOA)

The Equal Credit Opportunity Act (ECOA) Regulation B was instituted to protect applicants from discrimination throughout the credit process. It provides requirements to lenders for compliance. They shall not discriminate based on age, gender, ethnicity, nationality, marital status, or income from public assistance.

The two main aspects of Regulation B include:

- A creditor shall not discriminate against an applicant regarding any aspect of a credit transaction.

- A creditor shall not make any oral or written statement, in advertising or otherwise, to applicants or prospective applicants that would discourage, on a prohibited basis, a reasonable person from making or pursuing an application.

ECOA prohibits discrimination in all aspects of the mortgage process on the basis of all of the following:

- Gender
- Marital status (unless in a community property state)
- Age
- Race
- Ethnicity
- Religion
- Nationality
- Receipt of public assistance

Notice shall be provided within 30 days on an existing account to an applicant who is to be denied for a mortgage loan. The notice should include a statement of specific reasons for the denial including the credit agency which provided credit information.

There is information that is acceptable to be questioned under the act. These include:

- Immigration status
- Permanent residency
- Credit history
- May ask if a client is receiving child support or alimony

If a lender chooses to deny a loan application, the consumer has certain rights to information that must be disclosed These include:

- Reason for denial or informing the consumer that they have the right to request the reason for denial
- Notice of decision within 30 days of application
- Specific reasons for denial such as income or employment history
- Reasons for less favorable terms if offered
- Right to receive an appraisal if applicable
- Negative information from a credit report that influenced the decision

5. Mortgage fraud and predatory lending

Mortgage fraud is an attempt to provide false or incomplete information in order to obtain a loan or approval when the individual may otherwise not be qualified. Fraud may occur in a number of different aspects of the mortgage process including asset declaration, falsifying documentation such as contracts or applications, statement of income, employment fraud, and others. Applications and documents will be assessed for the presence of red flags which are indicators of fraud.

Asset fraud is a misrepresentation of assets to obtain a loan. The possible fraud indications can include:

- Asset Documentation
- Applicant's salary does not support savings on deposit
- Applicant does not use traditional banking institutions
- Pattern of loyalty to financial institutions other than the subject lender
- Balances are greater than the FDIC or SIPC insured limits
- Excessive balance maintained in checking account
- Dates of bank statements are unusual
- Recently deposited funds without a paper-trail or explanation
- Bank account ownership includes unknown parties
- Balances verified as even dollar amounts
- Two-month average balance is equal to present balance
- Source of earnest money is not apparent

Fannie Mae provides guidance on the potentially troubling aspects of a contract during review. Sales contract red flags include:

- Seller is not currently reflected on the title
- Purchaser is not the applicant
- Purchaser is deleted from or added to the sales contract
- No real estate agent is involved
- Power of attorney is used
- Second mortgage is indicated, but not disclosed on the application
- Earnest money deposit equals the entire down payment or is an odd amount for the local market
- Multiple deposit checks have inconsistent dates
- Name and/or address on earnest money deposit check differ from buyer's
- Real estate commission is excessive
- Contract dated after credit documents
- Contract is "boilerplate" with limited fill-in-the-blank terms, not reflective of a true negotiation

Mortgage Application fraud indicators include:

- Significant or contradictory changes from handwritten to typed application
- Unsigned or undated application
- Employer's address shown only as a post office box

- Loan purpose is cash-out refinance on a recently acquired property
- Buyer currently resides in the subject property
- Same telephone number for applicant and employer
- Extreme payment shock (may signal straw buyer and/ or inflated income)
- Purchaser of investment property does not own residence

Documentation and consistency are the keys to an underwriter verifying the information provided on an application is accurate as stated by the applicant. The amounts of income, assets, and liabilities shall be consistent across all bank statements, paystubs, accounts, and any other documentation.

Verification of gray areas may even be taken a step further. Certain actions that may be taken include contacting an employer to verify employment status or asking the applicant for a Letter of Explanation to provide further information and documentation on a questionable aspect of the application.

Employment and income documentation red flags include:

- Applicant's job title is generic, e.g., "manager," "vice president"
- Employer's address is a post office box, the property address, or the applicant's current residence
- Applicant's residence is in a location remote from the employer
- Employer name is similar to a party to the transaction
- Employer unable to be contacted
- Paystubs not consistent with assets
- Unusual or excessive amounts of overtime

There are two scenarios of fraud regarding the consumer's bank account. The first is fraudulent activity by the consumer and the second being activity taken against the consumer when the account has been compromised.

Activity by the consumer may include:

- Suspicious Cash Transactions
  - Deposits just below the reportable minimum
  - A number of deposits over a period of time below the reportable minimum
  - Suspicious transactions
- Check tampering
- Billing such as unexplainable reimbursements or fees

Fraud activity against the consumer can happen when the account has been compromised either by obtaining the consumer's personal information or by theft. These are usually identified by unusual transactions in different locations than the consumer is in.

Similarly, to income fraud, employment fraud red flags include:

- Applicant's job title is generic, e.g., "manager," "vice president"
- Employer's address is a post office box, the property address, or the applicant's current residence
- Applicant's residence is in a location remote from the employer
- Employer name is similar to a party to the transaction
- Employer unable to be contacted

Loan originators are required to report any suspicious activity that could jeopardize both the lender's investment and the applicant's wellbeing. If a financial institution suspects suspicious or illegal behavior, they must file a Suspicious Activity Report (SAR)

When a professional takes advantage of an ill-informed borrower for personal gain, this is called predatory lending. Loan types must be clearly and properly designated so that the consumer is not mislead into thinking a product is available or obtainable that is not.

Steering is forcing a specific geographical area on an applicant based on race, religion, or ethnicity and it is strictly prohibited.

D. Settlement and closing the transaction

Settlement is the finalizing of the loan. It is a meeting of the buyer, seller, and lender where the property and funds legally change hands. This is also referred to as closing. Documents to be provided at closing must include:

- Closing Disclosure (CD)
- Promissory Note
- Mortgage/Security Instrument/Deed of Trust
- Transfer of ownership for purchase transactions
- Right to Cancel
- Escrow statement

Closing disclosure provides the final costs and specifications of the loan. The information provided includes:

- Final interest rate
- Monthly payment
- Closing costs
- Cash to close

- Prepayment penalty
- Costs that may increase after closing
- Breakdown of closing costs
- Total cost of the loan
- APR
- Total interest paid over the life of the loan
- Late payment penalties
- Indication of negative amortization
- Loan assumption indication

The initial closing disclosure is the first one received after the underwriting approval. This must be provided 3 days prior to the signing of the final loan documents.

The closing disclosure must be provided 3 business days in advance of consummation.

The final closing disclosure details the final terms and costs of the loans. If nothing has changed, this will be the same as the initial CD. It must be provided 3 days prior to consummation.

Title insurance is paid as a one-time fee upfront and varies based on the value of the property and the anticipated work to secure the necessary title information.

Prepaids are payments that are required to be provided before they are due to the appropriate entity. Generally, for mortgages, this refers to the funding of escrow accounts including the property taxes, hazard insurance, and PMI. Lenders will often require that the escrow account includes a minimum amount of reserves to ensure there are sufficient funds in the account. The prepaids will include this buffer along with the required amount that will be needed at the time the bill is due.

At closing, there are often expenses related to establishing the escrow account. Generally, the funding of escrow accounts includes property taxes, hazard insurance, and PMI. Lenders will often require that the escrow account includes a minimum amount of reserves to ensure there are sufficient funds in the account. The prepaids will include this buffer along with the required amount that will be needed at the time the bill is due. A common amount of reserve is 3 months but may vary among lenders.

Origination fees are often a percentage of the purchase price, typically 1%. However, this can vary and there are instances where it is waived in return for a higher interest rate in which case the fee is paid by means of the yield spread premium.

Loan consummation is the time at which the borrower becomes contractually obligated to meet the agreement of the loan terms to the creditor. This is not necessarily the same as closing or settlement as different states may have different laws regarding when the obligation is final.

VIII. REAL ESTATE MATH CALCULATIONS (7)

A. Property area calculations

1. Square footage

Square footage is an area calculation used to determine the total size of the home. Rectangular rooms or homes can be determined by the length and width:

$$Square\ Footage = Length\ X\ Width$$

2. Acreage total

Acres are the standard unit of measure for the size of a lot of land. To convert between square footage and acres:

$$Acres = \frac{Square\ Footage}{43,560}$$

B. Property valuation

1. Comparative Market Analysis (CMA)

The market approach is the most common of the appraisal types and is used for most purchase loans. The value of the home is determined by comparison to other properties with similar characteristics that have been sold in as recent of a timeframe as possible. The comparisons (referred to as "comps") are then evaluated by identifying the differences in certain characteristics such as square footage, age, lot size, home type, street type, and many others. Typically, a minimum of three comps are required and the most similar and most recent homes are chosen. At times, homes that are currently on the market are also used as a basis for comparison but will not hold as much weight as the sales. If possible, homes no more than a 1-mile radius away from the home shall be chosen and as well as no more than 1 year prior to the transaction.

Once the comps are evaluated in comparison to the home to be purchased, the prices of the sales are adjusted to represent a price of equal value. These values are then averaged and evaluated using some appraiser judgment to determine a fair market value of the home.

2. Net Operating Income (NOI)

The income appraisal approach is a way of evaluating investment properties that will generate income. This is common for condo or apartment complexes where renters will reside. The approach involves calculating the Net Operating Income (NOI) which is the income generated divided by the capitalization rate:

$$NOI = \frac{Income}{Capitalization\ Rate}$$

3. Capitalization rate

The capitalization rate is a percentage representation of the expected income that can be generated from a property on a yearly basis if it is bought with a cash investment. It can be calculated as a function of the net operating income and the current market value of the property:

$$Capitalization\ Rate = \frac{NOI}{Market\ Property\ Value}$$

4. Equity in property

Equity is the amount of surplus value when the value of a property is compared to the outstanding amount on an existing loan. The property value can be determined as either the actual sale price or the appraised value of the home.

$$Amount\ of\ Equity = Property\ Value - Outstanding\ Loan\ Balance$$

5. Establishing a listing price

A listing price is agreed upon by the selling party and the listing agent. This is commonly arrived at by using a comparative market analysis taking into account recent comparable sales and current listings in the area.

6. Assessed value and property taxes

To calculate property tax, many states will use the millage rate equation:

$$Property\ Tax = \frac{Market\ Value\ of\ Property\ X\ Assessment\ Ratio\ X\ Millage\ Rate}{1000}$$

The millage rate is the tax rate applied to the assessed value. Millage rates are typically expressed per $1,000 with one mill representing $1 in tax for every $1,000.

C. Commission/compensation

Commission is based on the sales price of the home and can vary between typically between 4% - 6%. To determine the commission:

$$Commission = Sales\ Price\ X\ Commission\ Rate\ (as\ a\ decimal)$$

It is common practice for the seller to pay the fee but it can be negotiated or split as necessary.

D. Loan financing costs

1. Interest

Accrued interest is the amount of interest that has accumulated over a period of time since the inception of the loan or since the previous payment. For mortgages, this will be the amount of interest that has accrued each month in between payments. Accrued interest is determined based on the period in which the interest is calculated. For example, if daily interest is required, it will be calculated every day whereas monthly will be calculated once per month.

A periodic interest rate calculates interest based on the number of compounding periods. Lenders will typically quote interest rates based on an annual basis, but the compounding of the interest occurs most often at a monthly interval. This means that interest is being calculated at a rate of the annual divided by the number of compounding periods in a year. Be sure to convert the interest rate to decimal form by dividing by 100:

$$Interest = \frac{Rate\ in\ decimal\ form}{\#\ of\ compunding\ periods}\ x\ Principal\ Balance$$

Most often mortgages compound once per month or 12 times per year. So, the interest rate is divided by 12 to find the monthly interest.

Daily simple interest calculates interest on a daily basis as opposed to monthly like a traditional loan. To calculate, divide the annual rate by 365 days and multiply by the outstanding balance and then multiply by the number of days in the period:

$$Interest = \left(\frac{Annual\ Rate\ as\ a\ decimal}{365}\right)(Loan\ amount)(Number\ of\ days\ in\ period)$$

2. Loan to Value (LTV)

Loan-to-value ratio is the amount financed divided by the value of the home as determined either by the sale price for a purchase transaction or the appraised value for a refinance:

$$LTV = \frac{Amount\ of\ Loan}{Value\ of\ Property}$$

3. Fees

The settlement statement is a summary to identify all details costs and fees for the transaction. Fees and charges listed include:

- Broker/sales commissions
- Origination fee
- Loan discount
- Appraisal fee
- Credit report fee
- Lender's inspection fee
- Mortgage insurance application fee
- Assumption fee
- Items to be paid in advance
  - Taxes
  - Interest
  - Insurance
- Escrow reserves
- Title charges
- Recording and transfer fees
- Any additional fees not listed

Origination fees are often a percentage of the purchase price, typically 1%. However, this can vary and there are instances where it is waived in return for a higher interest rate in which case the fee is paid by means of the yield spread premium.

Prepaids are payments that are required to be provided before they are due to the appropriate entity. Generally, for mortgages, this refers to the funding of escrow accounts including the property taxes, hazard insurance, and PMI. Lenders will often require that the escrow account includes a minimum amount of reserves to ensure there are sufficient funds in the account. The prepaids will include this buffer along with the required amount that will be needed at the time the bill is due.

Title insurance is paid as a one-time fee upfront and varies based on the value of the property and the anticipated work to secure the necessary title information.

TILA-RESPA Integrated Disclosure Rule has 3 types of tolerance thresholds. This is to ensure a good faith standard of estimates and to allow the borrower to prepare for the required fees. The three types are:

- Zero tolerance: As the name implies there may be no increase from estimate to closing disclosure
- 10% cumulative tolerance: The change in all fees must not be more than 10%
- No or unlimited tolerance: Any change is acceptable

The 10% tolerance is a cumulation of all the fees. Fees subject to this are:

- All recording fees
- Third-party service fees which the borrower can shop for

4. Amortization, discount points, and prepayment penalties

Amortization schedules are used by lenders to present a loan repayment schedule based on specific loan characteristics. The schedule will identify the standing of the loan after each payment including the remaining principal balance, interest, and escrow payments.

Discount points allow the borrower an option to save money on interest over the life of the loan if they choose. The points are beneficial if the borrower will maintain the loan for a period of time that will exceed the breakeven point. This is when the savings from interest exceed the initial upfront cost of the points. Each point typically is worth 1% of the loan and lowers the interest rate by 0.25%.

Prepayment penalties are a choice for a lender to impose on a borrower. For prepayment penalties to be allowed, all of the following must be true:

- The APR must remain constant
- The loan is qualified
- The loan is not a higher-priced loan

Additionally, there are certain restrictions on penalties.

- A prepayment penalty is capped at 2% for the first two years and 1% thereafter.
- A prepayment penalty can only exist for the first 3 years

- The lender must offer a non-prepayment penalty loan option

E. Settlement and closing costs

1. Purchase price and down payment

Down payments are the amount of money provided by the borrower to make an initial payment against a loan. To calculate the down payment percentage, divide the amount of the down payment by the purchase price. Be careful to not use the loan amount:

$$\% \, Down \, Payment = \frac{Down \, Payment}{Purchase \, Price}$$

2. Monthly mortgage calculations- principal, interest, taxes, and insurance (PITI)

The monthly mortgage payment is calculated by the addition of all applicable aspects of the loan. This typically will include principal, interest, taxes, and insurance which is simplified as the acronym PITI for short. Additionally, the monthly payment may include PMI if applicable.

$$Monthly \, Payment = Principal + Interest + Taxes + Insurance + PMI$$

3. Net to the seller

When a property owner sells a home, they will either have a net gain or a net loss depending on the current amount of equity in the home and any fees incurred for the sale of the home. Typically, the seller is responsible for the sales commissions and some additional fees but others can be negotiated depending on the specific contract:

$$Net \, Gain \, or \, Loss = Sales \, Price - Outstanding \, loan - Seller \, Fees$$

4. Cost to the buyer

The cost to the buyer is the sales price plus any additional closing costs that they may incur for the purchase of the home. Closing costs include the expenses beyond the cost of the property itself that it takes to get the loan. Typically closing costs will range from 2%-5% of the purchase price of a loan.

$$Total \, Cost \, to \, the \, Buyer = Sales \, Price + Closing \, Costs$$

5. Prorated items

Due to the nature of tax payments in mortgages, there is a prorating of the costs incurred at closing. Tax payments are typically made twice annually but for a purchase agreement, the closing most likely occurs at some time in between these payments. The responsibilities of these taxes are then split between the seller and buyer based on the time since and until the payments. The seller will be responsible for everything up until closing and the buyer must pay everything beyond the closing date. Since the payment is already made, this may result in a credit between parties.

Interest is also a closing cost that is calculated on a prorated basis depending on the closing date. A seller is still responsible for the interest on a loan since their last payment. This interest accumulates daily. Interest per diem is a calculation of interest on a per-day basis:

$$Daily\ Interest\ for\ a\ Monthly\ Payment = \frac{rate}{365}\ x\ pricipal\ x\ number\ of\ days$$

6. Debits and credits

A debit is an entry of accounting that increases an asset or expense account, or decreases a liability or equity account. The simplest way to remember is debits identify money that flows into an account.

A credit is an entry of accounting that either increases a liability or equity account, or decreases an asset or expense account. Conversely to debits, credits identify money that is flowing out of and account.

7. Transfer tax and recording fee

A **transfer tax** on real estate is a fee imposed by state, county, or municipal law necessary to complete the transferring of real property. The amount of the tax is based on the property value and the property classification. Typically, the seller is liable for the real estate transfer tax, but it may be negotiated with the buyer.

A **recording fee** is a government fee imposed for registering or recording the purchase or sale of a piece of real estate. Recording fees are for the costs of the services provided by the clerk or recording agency that must maintain complete official documents.

F. Investment

1. Return on investment

The return on an investment (ROI) is the ratio of the net profit or loss upon sale of the asset. The factors included involve the purchase price, sale price, and any expenses incurred during the duration of ownership. Additionally, for investment or rental properties, there is the consideration of income received. Return on investment is often indicated as a percentage:

$$ROI = \frac{Net\ Return\ on\ Investment}{Cost\ of\ investment}\ x\ 100\%$$

2. Appreciation

Appreciation is the increase in value of an asset over time. Real estate is one of the few assets that do gain value as opposed to items such as most cars which lose value over time. Appreciation is only a function of value that is volatile and not guaranteed to go up. However, it can be approximated if a rate is determined. The average is often taken as 3.8% can vary by location. Appreciation can be calculated as follows for some time in the future:

$$Appreciated\ Home\ Value$$

$$= Sales\ Price\ X\ (1 + Yearly\ Rate\ of\ Appreciation\ (Decimal))^{Number\ of\ Years}$$

3. Depreciation

Depreciation is the loss of value over time for an asset. Depreciation is calculated by establishing a useful life of an asset and evenly reducing the original cost of the item on a yearly basis. While a property's value will typically appreciate over the life of its loan, depreciation can still be claimed for tax purposes on investment or rental properties. Additionally, depreciation can be claimed on these properties for improvements:

$$Depreciated\ Value = Original\ Sales\ Price - \#\ of\ Years\ X\ \left(\frac{Original\ Sales\ Price}{Useful\ Life}\right)$$

4. Tax implications on investment

The sale of real estate is treated as a capital gain or loss but is commonly an exempt transaction for the seller. The IRS has the following exemption amounts for net profit from a sale:

- $250,000 of capital gains on real estate for single filers.
- $500,000 of capital gains on real estate for married and filing jointly filers

Those who are not eligible for the exemption include:

- The home is not the owner's principal residence.
- The property owner lived in the home for less than two years in the five-year period before sale.
- The exemption was claimed on another home in the two-year period before the sale of this home.

- The home was purchased through a like-kind exchange.

The tax rate depends on the length of time the property was owned and the income level of the seller. A capital gain is considered short term if owned for less than one year and long term if owned for more than one year. The tax rate for long-term capital gains can be 0%, 15%, or 20% depending on the income.

G. Property management calculations

1. Property management and budget calculations

In real estate, an operating budget determines the income and expenses for a property. A property manager will prepare the annual operating budget for landlords and maintain it throughout the year. The budget is concerned with the gross operating income (GOI) and the operating expenses (OE) of the property. The income is generally from rental income but may include others such as interest or machines owned on the property that may generate income. The operating expenses are the costs to operate and maintain the property. These can be used to calculate the net operating income of the property:

$$\text{Net Operating Income } = \text{ Gross Operating Income } - \text{ Operating Expenses}$$

2. Tenancy and rental calculations

Rental calculations determine the loss or gain from ownership of a property with tenants. With the large amount of deductions, the net income may easily result in a loss despite having more income than expenses:

$$\text{Net Rental Income } = \text{ Gross Income } - \text{ Expenses } - \text{ Deductions}$$

Question 1

A corporation purchases a piece of land with a vacant warehouse. The building is to be repurposed for the construction of condominiums. What is the real estate classification of the purchase?

(A) Residential
(B) Commercial
(C) Industrial
(D) Special

Question 2

A homeowner purchases a house plant and keeps it in the bedroom of a new property. Eventually, the plant is taken outside and put into the ground. What is the most appropriate classification of the property?

(A) Real property
(B) Intangible property
(C) Land
(D) Chattel

Question 3

A business owner leases a building to open a restaurant. As a part of their operations, the owner installs large cooktops that are bolted to the ground in the proposed kitchen. The cooktops are classified as which of the following property types?

(A) Chattel
(B) Emblements
(C) Trade fixture
(D) Intangible property

Question 4

What characteristic of land can be classified as economic?

(A) Immobility
(B) Scarcity
(C) Uniqueness
(D) Indestructibility

Question 5

In a metes-and-bounds survey system, what statement is true regarding the point of ending (POE)?

(A) The POE must be established by a different landmark as the POB
(B) The POE may be estimated in relation to the POB
(C) The POE and the POB are the same identified point
(D) The POE does not need to be established

Question 6

The lot-and-block survey system:

(A) Must use the metes-and-bounds system to identify individual plots
(B) Must use the rectangular survey system to identify individual plots
(C) May use the rectangular survey system or metes and bounds to identify individual plots
(D) Independently identifies individual plots

Question 7

A survey can be used to identify all of the following except:

(A) Existing easements
(B) Environmental contaminants
(C) Property elevations
(D) Property hazards

Question 8

What incident listed below is an example of an encroachment on an owner's property?

(A) A portion of a fence built by a neighbor on the owner's property
(B) Governmental seizure of a portion of land adjacent to a construction site
(C) Purchase of a portion of land by a contractor for temporary use during construction
(D) Town enforcement of the removal of a fence due to safety regulations

Question 9

Covenants, conditions, and restrictions (CC&Rs) are applicable to which of the following property types?

(A) Multifamily homes
(B) Industrial properties
(C) Homes a part of a homeowner's association
(D) Commercial properties

Question 10

What is not a situation in which a property can be obtained or modified through the use of police power?

(A) Foreclosure
(B) Building code violations
(C) Tenant's rights violations
(D) Environmental regulations

Question 11

What type of real estate ownership legally views a couple as a single entity?

(A) Joint tenancy
(B) Tenancy in common
(C) Tenants by entirety
(D) Community property

Question 12

What fee simple type contains the automatic termination upon the occurrence of an identified event?

(A) Fee simple absolute
(B) Fee simple determinable
(C) Fee simple subject to a condition subsequent
(D) Fee simple subject to the executory limitation

Question 13

What is not one of the identified bundle of rights included upon transfer of the title?

(A) The right to possession
(B) The right to control
(C) The right to exclusion
(D) The right to termination

Question 14

What type of lease agreement does not require a written agreement between the tenant and the landlord?

(A) Estate for years
(B) Periodic estate
(C) Estate at will
(D) Estate at sufferance

Question 15

An estate at sufferance is established at what point?

(A) Upon the failure to make a payment by the tenant
(B) Upon expiration of the lease term but before notice to vacate
(C) Upon issuance of a notice to vacate
(D) Upon violation of the minimum amount of time identified in the notice to vacate

Question 16

A tenant and a landlord enter into a double net lease agreement. What are the payment responsibilities of the tenant?

(A) Rent only
(B) Rent and property tax
(C) Rent plus property taxes and insurance.
(D) Rent plus property taxes, insurance, and utilities

Question 17

A landlord and a tenant enter into a percentage lease at 10%. The property will house a restaurant run by the tenant. The rent agreed upon is $800 per month. In the month of January, the restaurant has a gross revenue of $5,000. What is the required payment to the landlord?

(A) $800
(B) $1,300
(C) $5,000
(D) $5,800

Question 18

A homeowner has an existing mortgage on a property that has a current outstanding balance of $150,000. A second mortgage is also taken out on the property with a current balance of $60,000. The homeowner becomes unable to pay their loans and the home is sold in foreclosure with proceeds totaling $170,000. What will be the remaining balance on the second mortgage after sale?

(A) $0
(B) $20,000
(C) $40,000
(D) $60,000

Question 19

What type of deed is used for the transfer of real estate between relatives where no exchange of money has taken place?

(A) Release
(B) Gift
(C) Fiduciary
(D) Bargain and sale

Question 20

What is not a requirement for the successful claim of adverse possession?

(A) Continuous use
(B) Actual possession
(C) Open and notorious possession
(D) Breach of current agreement

Question 21

A tenant is visited by a landlord at the property to discuss the terms of their lease. During the meeting, the landlord notices and comments on damage to the stairs to the basement. What type of notice is given to the landlord in regards to the need for the repair?

(A) Express actual notice
(B) Implied actual notice
(C) Constructive notice
(D) Legal notice

Question 22

A prospective buyer who has a large family will only buy a home with a minimum of five bedrooms. This requirement is an example of which characteristic of value?

(A) Demand
(B) Utility
(C) Purchasing power
(D) Transferability

Question 23

Which of the following appraisal types is most appropriate for an entire apartment complex?

(A) Market approach
(B) Income approach
(C) Cost approach
(D) None of the above

Question 24

Each of the options listed below indicates a characteristic of a different comparable property for a market appraisal, which is most likely to be omitted?

(A) Distance of 0.5 miles
(B) 200 square feet larger
(C) 35 years younger construction
(D) Sold 4 months ago

Question 25

What is not a prohibited practice related to obtaining an appraisal?

(A) Implying future work based on the valuation
(B) Indicating a minimum required valuation for a loan to be approved
(C) A consumer obtaining multiple appraisals
(D) Excluding payment if a valuation did not meet expectations

Question 26

What is the standard length of time over which a home is depreciated?

(A) 5 years
(B) 10.5 years
(C) 27.5 years
(D) 30 years

Question 27

A home sells for $200,000. The town has a millage rate of 14.8 and uses an 80% assessment ratio. Determine the property tax for the home.

(A) $2,368
(B) $3,380
(C) $4,555
(D) $6,800

Question 28

A home with 2,000 square feet is having a comparative market analysis performed. There are three comparative properties with price per square foot adjusted values of $200, $180, and $175. Determine the CMA value of the home.

(A) $280,000
(B) $320,000
(C) $370,000
(D) $420,000

Question 29

A property that has a gross annual rental income of $24,000 is being evaluated for sale. A comparable property has a gross annual rental income of $30,000 and sold for $280,000. Determine the comparable value of the property for sale.

(A) $224,000
(B) $255,000
(C) $280,000
(D) $310,000

Question 30

What is the reduction of a home's value due to outdated features that cannot be easily changed?

(A) Deterioration
(B) Depreciation
(C) Functional obsolescence
(D) Economic obsolescence

Question 31

The cost approach for appraisals is most likely appropriate for all of the following scenarios except:

(A) New construction
(B) Insurance
(C) Commercial
(D) Rental

Question 32

Total construction costs for a new home total $150,000. It is determined that depreciation is $5,000. If the land cost $45,000 determine the value of the home by the cost approach.

(A) $155,000
(B) $170,000
(C) $190,000
(D) $195,000

Question 33

If an express contract is established and agreed upon, an identical implied contract:

(A) Must be applied
(B) May be applied
(C) Cannot exist
(D) Supplements the express contract

Question 34

Real estate contracts can typically be classified as what type of contract?

(A) Unilateral
(B) Bilateral
(C) Option
(D) Adhesion

Question 35

Two parties have a dispute over a real estate contract. It is discovered in a court of law that there were errors in the contract. This would most likely deem the contract to be:

(A) Void
(B) Valid
(C) Voidable
(D) Unenforceable

Question 36

What type of contract termination is used for a material breach of contract?

(A) Termination for cause
(B) Termination for convenience
(C) Termination of performance
(D) Termination by means of prior agreement

Question 37

Upon completion of a real estate transaction, the interest the buyer gains in the property is called:

(A) Equitable title
(B) Mortgage interest
(C) Title insurance
(D) Title deed

Question 38

A buyer and seller agree to a sales price of $200,000. Included in the contract is an inspection contingency of 2%. What is the minimum amount of repair costs resulting from the inspection that initiates the contingency?

(A) $2,000
(B) $4,000
(C) $10,000
(D) $20,000

Question 39

The agent's requirement to follow directions from the client and fulfill these needs is the requirement for which licensee obligation?

(A) Loyalty
(B) Accounting
(C) Obedience
(D) Confidentiality

Question 40

Time is of the essence is a contractual obligation that requires a party to act:

(A) In a reasonable timeframe
(B) In a specified timeframe
(C) In a reasonable or specified timeframe
(D) Without any restrictions on timetables

Question 41

What is most likely not an item negotiated as a part of a counteroffer?

(A) Closing costs
(B) Earnest money amount
(C) Closing date
(D) None of the above

Question 42

What is the maximum amount of seller concessions for an FHA loan?

(A) 2%
(B) 3%
(C) 6%
(D) 10%

Question 43

What is an advantage to the seller in the use of an installment sales contract?

(A) The seller retains possession of the property
(B) The gains are spread out over the life of the loan to reduce capital gain taxes
(C) The seller has the ability to attract a larger pool of buyers
(D) The seller receives all gains in a lumps sum payment

Question 44

Two parties agree to an option contract. Once the property becomes available, what is the obligation of the buyer?

(A) The buyer is alerted first to the availability but must bid against other buyers
(B) The buyer has exclusive rights to buy the property in perpetuity
(C) The buyer has first right of refusal to buy the property
(D) The buyer has allowed the purchase to be made by another party

Question 45

A buyer and a brokerage agree to a net listing agreement. The baseline price is set at $150,000. If the home sells for $170,000, what is the commission amount for the agent?

(A) $0
(B) $10,000
(C) $20,000
(D) $30,000

Question 46

What listing agreement between a buyer and broker does not include listing the home on the MLS?

(A) Exclusive right to sell listing
(B) Exclusive agency listing
(C) Open listing
(D) Net listing

Question 47

Which of the following is not exempted from the Fair Housing Act?

(A) Rental of a room in a dwelling with no more than four independent units
(B) Housing operated by private organizations
(C) Housing operated by private clubs
(D) Multi-family home without the use of a broker or real estate agent

Question 48

A real estate agent encourages a borrower to lie about their income so that they may be able to afford a more expensive home leading to a higher fee for the transaction. This can be classified as which of the following?

(A) Predatory lending
(B) Steering
(C) Bait and switch
(D) Redlining

Question 49

What Title of the Americans with Disabilities Act applies to disabled individuals seeking employment?

(A) I
(B) II
(C) III
(D) IV

Question 50

What is a true statement regarding the ability of a real estate professional to join MLS?

(A) A professional can join more than one region
(B) A professional can only have access to a single region
(C) MLS is a singular national database
(D) MLS is in the public domain and may be accessed by anyone

Question 51

What is not an example of non-public information?

(A) Phone number from a telephone book
(B) Social security provided through a financial service
(C) Information obtained through internet cookies
(D) Credit score

Question 52

A buyer has a home inspection done on a property. The inspection identifies the roof as being very old and in need of repair. If the buyer suggests that the seller share the cost of repair for the roof, what type of risk management strategy is being employed?

(A) Avoidance
(B) Reduction
(C) Transference
(D) Acceptance

Question 53

A mortgage lender that advertises a low-interest rate that is unattainable and instead tries to sell products in which are costlier is performing which of the following techniques?

(A) Bandwagon advertising
(B) Steering
(C) Bait and switch
(D) Shock advertising

Question 54

A broker represents a seller who owns a piece of land. A contractor wishes to buy the land to build homes. The brokerage informs the contractor that they can only buy the land if they can represent the contractor when it comes time to sell. What antitrust prohibition is the brokerage in violation of?

(A) Price fixing
(B) Group boycotting
(C) The allocation of market
(D) Tie-in agreement

Question 55

A title search comes back with an indication that the local railroad company has the ability to access part of the home's land for access to the tracks. This can be classified as which of the following issues resulting from the title search?

(A) Lien
(B) Encumbrance
(C) Easement
(D) Survey dispute

Question 56

Which of the following is not one of the three prohibitions as per the Gramm-Leach Bliley Act?

(A) Right to Access
(B) Financial Privacy
(C) Safeguard Rule
(D) Pretexting Prohibition

Question 57

To avoid prohibited steering, what is not an example of a required loan type that must be presented to the consumer?

(A) The loan with the lowest interest rate
(B) The loan with the lowest interest rate without a prepayment penalty
(C) The loan with the lowest total dollar amount
(D) The loan with the lowest origination fees

Question 58

What duty most likely falls outside of the scope of property management?

(A) Accounting
(B) Eviction
(C) Property showings
(D) Performing repairs

Question 59

During the life of a loan, FEMA has determined that a property that was previously in the moderate-risk flood zone, is now in a high-risk flood zone. Which of the following statements is true regarding the requirements for flood insurance?

(A) FEMA now requires the property to get flood insurance
(B) FEMA allows a 10-year grace period until the property is required to get flood insurance
(C) The property is grandfathered in and does not require flood insurance
(D) FEMA recommends flood insurance, but it is not required

Question 60

Which of the following is most likely eligible to be covered by errors and omissions insurance?

(A) Monetary loss due to mistakes during the closing
(B) Legal fees related to prohibited advertising practices
(C) Damage caused by the agent to a listed property
(D) Hospital bills to an injured individual during a showing

Question 61

Which of the following statement is most likely false regarding a brownfield site?

(A) The site may be revitalized for sale and use
(B) The site contains the presence or potential presence of hazardous materials
(C) The site falls under the EPA Land Revitalization Program
(D) The site has Federal oversight

Question 62

Disclosure requirements are determined by which of the following?

(A) Federal requirements
(B) State requirements
(C) The selling agent
(D) The seller

Question 63

What is not a change to the Comprehensive Environmental Response, Compensation, and Liability Act (CERCLA) as per the Superfund Amendments and Reauthorization Act?

(A) Allowed the EPA to identify guilty parties and force aid in cleanup
(B) Increased State involvement
(C) Revised the Hazard Ranking System
(D) Stressed the importance of permanent remedies and innovative treatment technologies in cleaning up hazardous waste sites

Question 64

In what year was asbestos banned as a construction material?

(A) 1950
(B) 1965
(C) 1978
(D) 1985

Question 65

Soil sampling is most likely to be associated with which environmental site assessment phase?

(A) I
(B) II
(C) III
(D) IV

Question 66

What is not a function of the CFPB?

(A) Conduct research on consumer behavior
(B) Investigate consumer complaints
(C) Alert consumers to possible risks
(D) Dictate recommended consumer actions

Question 67

Which of the following types of loans is it acceptable to have a 0% down payment?

(A) Conventional
(B) VA
(C) FHA
(D) None of the above

Question 68

Which of the following entities cannot be considered a part of the primary mortgage market?

(A) Mortgage bankers
(B) Mortgage brokers
(C) Credit unions
(D) Mortgage aggregator

Question 69

An FHA loan is to be used for a purchase in an area deemed to be classified as the lowest cost market. In 2019, the FHA ceiling is $726,525 and the floor is $314,827. What is the loan limit for the FHA mortgage in this county?

(A) $314,827
(B) $500,000
(C) 110% of the median sale price
(D) $726,525

Question 70

At what loan-to-value percentage will PMI be automatically removed on a conventional loan?

(A) 75%
(B) 78%
(C) 80%
(D) 90%

Question 71

An advertisement uses the term "fixed" to describe a rate for a non-variable rate transaction where the payment will increase in a stepped fashion. According to the Truth in Lending Act, which of the following must accompany the term "fixed" in the advertisement in close proximity?

(A) The term "Variable Rate Mortgage"
(B) The term "Fixed Rate Mortgage"
(C) The term "ARM"
(D) The time period for which the payment is fixed

Question 72

Which of the following fee tolerance thresholds permit a 0% increase in fees from the loan estimate to the closing disclosure?

(A) Zero tolerance
(B) 10% cumulative tolerance
(C) no or unlimited tolerance
(D) Tiered tolerance

Question 73

If the consumer does not provide an intent to proceed, how long does it take in days for the initial loan estimate to expire?

(A) 10
(B) 15
(C) 21
(D) 30

Question 74

A borrower owns a home valued at $450,000 and owes $300,000. He wishes to obtain a Home Equity Line of Credit. The lender is allowing access up to 90% of equity. What is the maximum amount of the HELOC loan?

(A) $50,000
(B) $75,000
(C) $105,000
(D) $150,000

Question 75

A simple-interest mortgage has a rate of 4.0% and a current balance of $100,000. What is the interest due at the end of a 30-day period?

(A) $225
(B) $329
(C) $380
(D) $425

Question 76

On a loan estimate, a borrower has total closing costs of $8200. The down payment will be $19,500. If a deposit of $5000 was provided previously, calculate the estimated cash to close.

(A) $11300
(B) $19500
(C) $22700
(D) $27700

Question 77

A proposed loan amount of $300,000 will have an interest rate of 4.25%. However, the borrower chooses to buy 2 points on the loan for a lower interest rate. What is the new interest rate?

(A) 3.75%
(B) 4.00%
(C) 4.50%
(D) 4.75%

Question 78

A borrower has an adjustable-rate mortgage with an initial fixed rate of 5.0%. At the time the fixed rate expires, the index is determined to be 3% and the margin is 2.5%. If the outstanding balance on the loan is $158,000, what is the increase in the monthly interest-only for the first month of the adjustable rate?

(A) $65.83
(B) $95.66
(C) $101.22
(D) $145.90

Question 79

Calculate the required prepaid costs on a loan estimate. The property tax requirement is 3 months at an annual cost of $5000/year. The homeowner's insurance requirement is 6 months at a rate of $1100/year and there are 10 days of interest required at 17.25 per day at a rate of 4.5%.

(A) $1972
(B) $2025
(C) $2200
(D) $2435

Question 80

A borrower has an existing mortgage principal of $230,000 on a home that is valued at $280,000. The borrower wishes to purchase a second home at a total cost of $220,000. What percent down on the second home must the borrower put to keep the combined LTV at 80%?

(A) 15%
(B) 18%
(C) 20%
(D) 23%

Question 81

What real estate classification covers governmental owned buildings for public services?

(A) Residential
(B) Commercial
(C) Industrial
(D) Special

Question 82

What example of personal property below is most likely to be identified as a fixture?

(A) Furnace
(B) Light fixture
(C) Toaster
(D) House plant

Question 83

What factor is not a consideration in the determination of classifying an item of property as a fixture?

(A) Minimum purchase price of the property
(B) Nature of the attachment to the property
(C) Inclusion in the original construction
(D) Terms of the purchase agreement

Question 84

A bill of sale shall include all of the following elements except:

(A) Date of purchase
(B) Description of asset transferred
(C) Amount paid for asset
(D) Qualifications of purchaser

Question 85

A homeowner has decided to put her home up for sale. Before doing so, she decides to make some improvements to the home including an electrical upgrade. Which economic characteristic of land does the homeowner affect which will influence the value of the property?

(A) Scarcity
(B) Location
(C) Permanence of investment
(D) Indestructibility

Question 86

What is not one of the three methods for the description of a property

(A) Graphical positioning system
(B) Metes-and-bounds
(C) Lot-and-block
(D) Rectangular survey

Question 87

In a metes-and-bounds survey system, a mete is defined as which of the following elements?

(A) Point of beginning
(B) The boundary lines between identified points
(C) The enclosed are
(D) Point of ending

Question 88

A Covenants, conditions, and restrictions (CC&Rs) agreement may include any of the following except:

(A) Changes made to the property
(B) Parking restrictions
(C) Changes in square footage to a property
(D) Mortgage prepayment penalties

Question 89

When a property is taken by eminent domain, what is the required amount of compensation to the property owner?

(A) The owner does not need to receive compensation
(B) The assessed property value
(C) Fair market value
(D) The most recent sale price

Question 90

Escheat is the right of the government to seize which of the following types of property?

(A) Properties in violation of environmental laws
(B) Foreclosures
(C) Properties suspected of housing illegal activities
(D) Unclaimed properties

Question 91

A property owner has a piece of land that is identified as needed for a governmental project. The homeowner does not wish to sell and eminent domain has been initiated. Which of the following is a violation of the homeowner's rights?

(A) Ability to challenge the need for the project in the interest of public good
(B) Ability to challenge the offer of fair market value
(C) Ability to seek legal counsel
(D) Ability to no longer maintain the property

Question 92

What type of real estate ownership allows for unequal ownership of the property?

(A) Joint tenancy
(B) Tenancy in common
(C) Tenants by entirety
(D) Community property

Question 93

What fee simple type allows for the option of termination upon the occurrence of an identified event?

(A) Fee simple absolute
(B) Fee simple determinable
(C) Fee simple subject to a condition subsequent
(D) Fee simple subject to the executory limitation

Question 94

Which right in the bundle of rights identifies the titleholder as the legal owner of the property?

(A) The right of possession
(B) The right of control
(C) The right of exclusion
(D) The right of disposition

Question 95

In an established life estate for a property, the life tenant wishes to sell the property What statement is true regarding the ability of the life tenant to sell the property?

(A) The life tenant has full rights to sell the property
(B) The remainderman has full rights to sell the property
(C) The property cannot be sold
(D) The life tenant can sell the property only with the consent of the remainderman

Question 96

A landlord has an established estate at will agreement with a tenant but without a written contract. What is the legal requirement for notice to vacate?

(A) There is no requirement since no agreement has been established
(B) Only the landlord is required to provide notice to vacate
(C) Only the tenant must provide notice to vacate
(D) Both the landlord and the tenant must provide notice of intent to vacate

Question 97

A tenant and a landlord enter into a triple net lease agreement. The costs incurred on a particular month are as follows:

- Rent: $900
- Property Taxes: $300
- Insurance: $90
- Utilities: $150

What is the total responsibility of the tenant?

(A) $900
(B) $1,200
(C) $1,290
(D) $1,440

Question 98

Which of the following statements are true regarding the payout of proceeds on a single property with multiple liens?

(A) The proceeds get distributed evenly
(B) The proceeds only go to the highest priority lien despite the amount of proceeds
(C) All liens must receive a minimum amount of the proceeds
(D) The proceeds may be exhausted before all parties receive payment

Question 99

A property owner purchases a home and later discovers there is a rare mineral in the ground under the surface of the property. The title has no noted restrictions to ownership of the subsurface. Who has claim to ownership of the minerals?

(A) The property owner
(B) The local government
(C) The public
(D) The previous owner

Question 100

What type of deed only warrants any title defect from the time the grantor took possession of the property, but not prior?

(A) Quitclaim
(B) Limited warranty
(C) Fiduciary
(D) Grant

Question 101

A governmental entity is to take a property by means of escheat. The information is provided in multiple newspapers indicating the lack of any identifiable heir. What type of notice is being provided for the acquisition of the property?

(A) Express actual notice
(B) Implied actual notice
(C) Constructive notice
(D) Legal notice

Question 102

What title recording tracks the detailed chain of ownership back to the original owner?

(A) Abstract of title
(B) Chain of title
(C) Market of title
(D) Cloud on title

Question 103

A property owner wishes to sell their home. The seller is having difficulty finding a suitable buyer due to the high value of the property limiting the pool of potential buyers. This limitation is an example of which characteristic of value?

(A) Demand
(B) Scarcity
(C) Purchasing power
(D) Transferability

Question 104

Which of the following appraisal types is most appropriate for a school building?

(A) Market approach
(B) Income approach
(C) Cost approach
(D) None of the above

Question 105

Which of the following is not considered a valid valuation as determined by ECOA?

(A) An appraiser's report
(B) A report by a government-sponsored entity
(C) A broker opinion price
(D) Any publicly available valuation

Question 106

Which of the following is not a violation of ensuring appraiser independence?

(A) Encouraging a targeted value
(B) Withholding appraiser payment
(C) Providing further detail for consideration
(D) Mischaracterization of the property

Question 107

What is not a true statement regarding a broker price opinion (BPO)?

(A) A BPO is a value based on expert judgment and not an official valuation
(B) The BPO can be done quicker and cheaper than an assessment
(C) A BPO is based off of qualitative neighborhood characteristics
(D) The BPO may be used to determine the assessed value

Question 108

A comparative market analysis is being performed. One of the comparable properties has a square footage of 1,500 sq. ft. and the home being evaluated has a total area of 1,800 sq. ft. If the adjustment for living area is $1,000 per 100 square feet, what is the adjustment in the comparable property's value?

(A) -$1,000
(B) -$3,000
(C) +$1,000
(D) +$3,000

Question 109

The gross income multiplier is calculated using which of the following values?

(A) Annual net income
(B) Annual gross income
(C) The depreciated operating income
(D) The lifespan income

Question 110

What method of the cost approach to appraisals includes construction costs based on a new structure with newer materials, current construction methods, and design?

(A) Reclamation
(B) Replacement
(C) Reproduction
(D) Recovery

Question 111

What is not one of the identified required elements of a valid contract?

(A) Offer
(B) Intention
(C) Timely
(D) Capacity

Question 112

A real estate contract is considered actionable. However, it is discovered in the later stages the process that crucial information was purposefully withheld. The contract is most likely considered:

(A) Void
(B) Valid
(C) Voidable
(D) Unenforceable

Question 113

A real estate contract required the delivery of an appraisal by a specified date. The party responsible provides it a day late. What type of breach of contract is this?

(A) Material
(B) Minor
(C) Anticipatory
(D) Actual

Question 114

The legal payments imposed on a defendant found guilty is:

(A) Liquidated damages
(B) Punitive damages
(C) Liability cost
(D) Compensatory damages

Question 115

A buyer and a seller agree to a contractual clause that provides the seller with 3% of the purchase price if the buyer is in breach of a contract. What type of damages are agreed to?

(A) Liquidated damages
(B) Punitive damages
(C) Liability cost
(D) Compensatory damages

Question 116

A seller has a contract with a buyer for the purchase of real estate. The seller is informed that the buyer intends to not attend the closing. At the time the information is known, what type of breach of contract is being performed?

(A) Minor
(B) Material
(C) Anticipatory
(D) Fundamental

Question 117

If recission is applied to a contract, what is the state of the agreement between the parties?

(A) The contract may resume as agreed upon
(B) The obligations of each party return to the point before the breach of contract occurred
(C) The obligations of each party resume without the identified item which caused the breach of contract
(D) The contact is treated as if never executed

Question 118

The use of a kick-out clause:

(A) Allows the seller to take another offer without notifying the seller
(B) Allows the seller to take another offer but the buyer is allowed to match
(C) Allows the seller to take another offer that is less than the current offer only
(D) Prevents the seller from taking any additional offers on the property

Question 119

A real estate agent comes to an agreement to represent a buyer in the sale of a single home. What type of client relationship is the representation?

(A) General agent
(B) Universal agent
(C) Special agent
(D) None of the above

Question 120

What statement is true regarding the legality of implied agency relationships?

(A) Agency must have a written contract
(B) Agency does not need a written contract
(C) The need for a written contract varies by state law
(D) Both implied or written agency is acceptable everywhere

Question 121

If a counteroffer is provided, what is the status of the original offer made?

(A) The original offer still stands
(B) The original offer still stands and must be addressed
(C) The original offer still stands if the counteroffer is rejected
(D) The original offer is now void

Question 122

Seller concessions for conventional loans are limited based on what factor?

(A) Down payment
(B) Purchase price
(C) Contingencies
(D) LTV ratio

Question 123

Interest rates for seller financing loans are:

(A) Determined by national averages
(B) Determined by an underwriter
(C) Provided by the financial institution
(D) Negotiated between the buyer and seller

Question 124

The price of the property or home set in an option contract is:

(A) A fixed purchase price
(B) A maximum allowable price
(C) A minimum purchase price
(D) Subject to a predetermined range

Question 125

What is an example of a real estate agent working outside of the scope of their duties?

(A) Providing service recommendations
(B) Legal advice
(C) Providing a sale price
(D) Suggest counter offers

Question 126

What statement is true for an exclusive agency listing but not for an exclusive right to sell brokerage agreement?

(A) The seller can't hire another broker
(B) The brokerage has exclusive rights to sell the home
(C) Brokerage is only paid if they bring in the buyer
(D) The agreement is for a specified timeframe

Question 127

What is not an acceptable use of a security deposit by a landlord?

(A) Cover the cost of repairs
(B) Replace unpaid rent
(C) Cleaning the property left in unsatisfactory conditions
(D) Cover costs of improvements to the home

Question 128

The Fair Housing Act requires all of the following to be provided in advertising except:

(A) Include a sentence explanation of the Fair Housing Act in all advertisements
(B) Include the "equal housing lender" slogan in any broadcast advertisement
(C) Display and Equal Housing Opportunity poster wherever mortgage loans are made
(D) Display the Equal Housing Opportunity Logo on all printed promotional material

Question 129

Which of the following is the practice of channeling prospective buyers to specific neighborhoods based on race, religion, or ethnicity?

(A) Steering
(B) Blockbusting
(C) Redlining
(D) Predatory lending

Question 130

What statement below is false regarding the Multiple Listing Service (MLS)?

(A) Access to MLS requires paid dues
(B) MLS is not available to the general public
(C) Sellers can post their home to MLS without an agent but not access other homes for sale
(D) MLS is divided into regional service

Question 131

What regulation does not have requirements against the discrimination of individuals in a real estate transaction?

(A) Fair Housing Act
(B) Civil Rights Act
(C) Home Mortgage Disclosure Act
(D) Exemption Act

Question 132

A real estate agent has a home office. A client in a wheelchair agrees to representation but the agent does not have a ramp compliant with the Americans with Disabilities Act. What statement applies to the agent's responsibilities?

(A) The agent is in violation of Title I of the ADA
(B) The agent is in violation of Title III of the ADA
(C) Home offices do not need to comply with the ADA
(D) The ramp is too expensive and therefore falls outside of ADA requirements

Question 133

Before a financial institution can disclose nonpublic information to a third party, what is not a requirement that must be provided to the consumer?

(A) An initial notice of the institution's privacy policies
(B) An opt-out notice
(C) Identification of the third party
(D) A reasonable time frame to opt-out

Question 134

What is the minimum number of employees at a real estate sales office in which Title I of the ADA Act applies?

(A) 0
(B) 5
(C) 10
(D) 15

Question 135

Which of the following is not a typical trait of a borrower who can be classified as subprime?

(A) History of a foreclosure
(B) Debt to income ratio of 40% or more
(C) FICO score below 600
(D) History of bankruptcy

Question 136

To prevent illegal flipping, FHA requires purchasers to own a home for how long before selling again?

(A) 3 months
(B) 6 months
(C) 1 year
(D) 2 years

Question 137

Risks may be identified as:

(A) Threats only
(B) Opportunities only
(C) Threats or opportunities
(D) Neither threats nor opportunities

Question 138

A real estate agent who works for a broker is representing a seller. The seller tells the agent of water damage that has occurred in the basement but the real estate agent tells the seller that they should agree to not disclose the information. Later on, the brokerage is sued for nondisclosure. The brokerage is subject to which of the following?

(A) General liability
(B) Vicarious liability
(C) Malpractice
(D) The brokerage is not responsible for the actions of the agent

Question 139

As per FEMA flood insurance requirements, the amount of coverage must be the lesser of all of the following except:

(A) The maximum amount of NFIP coverage available for the particular property type
(B) The appraised value of the property
(C) The outstanding principal balance of the loan
(D) The insurable value of the structure

Question 140

The agreement to divide areas with customers so that there is no competition within markets is what antitrust prohibition?

(A) Price fixing
(B) Group boycotting
(C) The allocation of market
(D) Tie-in agreement

Question 141

As per EPA definitions, what is the minimum amount of underground volume for a storage tank to be considered underground?

(A) 10%
(B) 25%
(C) 50%
(D) 75%

Question 142

During a property walkthrough it is observed that water is seeping though the walls of the foundation causing a moist condition in the basement. The home is built in 1980. What hazardous substance is most likely to be present?

(A) Asbestos
(B) Lead paint
(C) Mold
(D) Radon

Question 143

A Phase I environmental site assessment is used to achieve what goal?

(A) Determine the likelihood of a site contamination
(B) Test for the presence of contamination
(C) Determines an action plan for identified contamination
(D) Determines the cost of remediation for site contamination

Question 144

What is the generally accepted action level established by the World Health Organization for levels of radon in pCi/L?

(A) 1.5 pCi/L
(B) 2.7 pCi/L
(C) 3.5 pCi/L
(D) 4.2 pCi/L

Question 145

According to RESPA, what is the maximum allowable "cushion" for a borrower's escrow account that a lender can require?

(A) 1/12 of yearly disbursements
(B) 1/6 of yearly disbursements
(C) 1% of the total loan
(D) 3% of the total loan

Question 146

As per ECOA, a creditor is able to consider the inclusion of a source of income based on which of the following?

(A) Part-time vs full-time income
(B) Income from a pension
(C) Probability of continuance
(D) Income from alimony

Question 147

Which of the following mortgage types are 100% government insured?

(A) VA
(B) FHA
(C) USDA
(D) Conventional

Question 148

A balloon loan is most appropriate for which of the following scenarios?

(A) A borrower with a high down payment amount
(B) A borrower who will be moving in 2 years
(C) A borrower with a poor credit score
(D) Purchase of a second property

Question 149

What is the minimum credit score needed to be able to provide a down payment of less than 10% on an FHA loan?

(A) 500
(B) 550
(C) 580
(D) 620

Question 150

What is the front-end and back-end maximum qualifying FHA debt ratios?

(A) 28/40
(B) 31/43
(C) 35/48
(D) 38/50

Question 151

As per the ECOA, the applicant is not required to submit which of the following forms of income?

(A) Reliable alimony
(B) Part-time jobs
(C) Public assistance income
(D) Social Security income

Question 152

Which of the following is a true statement regarding the function of Private Mortgage Insurance?

(A) PMI protects the lender in case of borrower failure to pay
(B) PMI protects the lender and borrower in case of borrower failure to pay
(C) PMI protects the borrower in case of borrower failure to pay
(D) PMI supplements hazard insurance in case of damage

Question 153

How many business days after the receipt of a loan application must the initial loan estimate be provided?

(A) 3
(B) 7
(C) 10
(D) 30

Question 154

A loan amount is $200,000. The total amount of interest that will be paid over the loan term is $100,000. Calculate the Total Interest Percentage (TIP).

(A) 25%
(B) 50%
(C) 75%
(D) 100%

Question 155

For a conventional loan where the down payment is 12% for an investment property, what is the maximum amount of seller-paid concessions for the transaction?

(A) 2%
(B) 3%
(C) 6%
(D) 9%

Question 156

A seller agent and a buyer agent agree to a commission split. The total commission will be 6% on a $350,000 home. What is the commission for the seller's agent?

(A) $8,250
(B) $10,500
(C) $15,550
(D) $21,000

Question 157

What is the maximum amount of a prepayment penalty for the first two years of the life of a loan?

(A) 1%
(B) 2%
(C) 3%
(D) 5%

Question 158

A borrower must keep his debt-to-income ratio at 40% maximum. She has $500 and $300 per month in credit card payments and student loans respectively. What is the maximum allowable monthly total mortgage payment if her monthly gross income is $5750?

(A) $1200
(B) $1500
(C) $2000
(D) $2200

Question 159

A mortgage applicant is provided with a loan estimate that includes $5000 in recording fees and is subject to the 10% cumulative fee limit. What is the maximum amount for the recording fees that are acceptable on the closing disclosure?

(A) $5000
(B) $5200
(C) $5450
(D) $5500

Question 160

A mortgage applicant has a yearly salary of $60,000/year. The home he wishes to purchase has a monthly tax bill of $450/month, insurance of $90/month, and PMI of $120/month. What is the maximum mortgage amount to keep the housing ratio to 28% or less?

(A) $740
(B) $890
(C) $1100
(D) $1350

Question 161

Which of the following is most likely not classified as real property?

(A) Trees
(B) Sheds
(C) Crops
(D) Shrubs

Question 162

All of the following can be classified as a chattel except:

(A) Furniture
(B) Clothing
(C) Flowers
(D) Patents

Question 163

A business owner leases a property to open a new bar. The tenant makes modifications to the property including installation of larger items for the proper functioning of the bar. Which of the following are true statements regarding the ownership of the installation of trade fixtures?

(A) The fixtures become owned by the landlord once installed
(B) The fixtures remain the property of the tenant
(C) The fixtures are the property of the tenant as long as they remain removable
(D) The fixtures can be claimed by either party

Question 164

All of the following can be classified as natural attachments except:

(A) Pond
(B) Shrub
(C) Well
(D) Flowers

Question 165

What statement below is true regarding the terms of a bill of sale?

(A) A bill of sale always provides an absolute transfer of ownership
(B) A bill of sale always provides a conditional transfer of ownership
(C) A bill of sale may provide an absolute or conditional transfer of ownership
(D) None of the above

Question 166

What characteristic of land can be classified as physical?

(A) Immobility
(B) Location preference
(C) Indestructibility
(D) Uniqueness

Question 167

The property taxes are determined based on which of the following?

(A) Assessed value and millage rate
(B) Assessed value and local state sales tax
(C) Appraised value and the millage rate
(D) Appraised value and the local state sales tax

Question 168

What is a true statement regarding the difference between police power and eminent domain?

(A) Police power requires compensation to the owner while eminent domain does not
(B) Police power does not require compensation to the owner while eminent domain does
(C) Both police power and eminent domain require compensation to the owner
(D) Neither police power nor eminent domain require compensation to the owner

Question 169

In general, zoning ordinances are determined by which of the following entities?

(A) Federal government
(B) State government
(C) Municipal government
(D) Home owner's association

Question 170

A governmental project is initiated to install a pipeline. The proposed line will need to go underground through an individual property owner's land but will be 10 feet underground. The landowner is not amenable and does not wish to sell the rights to build under the land. What statement is true regarding the government's ability to obtain the necessary rights to build?

(A) The government may institute police power to obtain the property
(B) The government must use eminent domain to obtain the entire property
(C) The government may use eminent domain to obtain an easement to build underground
(D) The government may not obtain the necessary rights

Question 171

What type of real estate ownership is not available in all states?

(A) Sole
(B) Joint
(C) Common
(D) Community

Question 172

What type of fee simple is not dependent on a conditional requirement?

(A) Fee simple absolute
(B) Fee simple determinable
(C) Fee simple subject to a condition subsequent
(D) Fee simple defeasible

Question 173

The bundle of rights is afforded to an individual in which of the following steps of the home buying process?

(A) Agreement with broker
(B) Approval by underwriter
(C) Acceptance of offer by the seller
(D) Transfer of title

Question 174

A property owner establishes a life estate naming a beneficiary. Upon death of the life tenant, the property shall be transferred to which of the following?

(A) The grantor
(B) The financial institution
(C) The remainderman
(D) The life tenant's next of kin

Question 175

A property owner and a tenant agree to a lease. It is determined that the tenant will live in the property for a specified amount of time and no more than the established end date. What type of agreement is established?

(A) Estate for years
(B) Periodic estate
(C) Estate at will
(D) Estate at sufferance

Question 176

What type of lease agreement includes all costs incurred during the tenancy to be the responsibility of the tenant?

(A) Gross
(B) Net
(C) Percentage
(D) None of the above

Question 177

Title insurance covers:

(A) The lender only
(B) The borrower only
(C) The lender and the borrower
(D) The government on backed loans

Question 178

What is not one of the three guarantees of a general warranty deed?

(A) The grantor owns the title free and clear of any defects
(B) No one will make a claim against the property
(C) There are no liens or encumbrances other than stated in the deed
(D) The grantor will defend the title of the property against third-party claims

Question 179

What type of involuntary alienation is the term for the loss of land due to natural causes?

(A) Avulsion
(B) Partitioning
(C) Aversion
(D) Forfeiture

Question 180

A marketable title is one that:

(A) Includes guarantee that the title is free of mistakes
(B) The title cannot be brought to court for legal dispute
(C) May include mistakes but shall be legally viable
(D) Includes mistakes that need to be addressed before transfer

Question 181

A closing protection letter is a document that is provided in association with which of the following?

(A) Abstract of title
(B) Opinion of title
(C) Chain of title
(D) Title insurance

Question 182

What is not one of the identified characteristics of market value?

(A) Demand
(B) Flexibility
(C) Scarcity
(D) Utility

Question 183

A property is bought and the appraisal is artificially inflated. The home is resold shortly after purchase at a profit. Which of the following illegal tactics is likely being employed?

(A) Redlining
(B) Flipping
(C) Mortgage fraud
(D) Coercion

Question 184

As per ECOA, a mortgage applicant must be informed of the right to receive an appraisal within _____ business days of the receipt of the application.

(A) 3
(B) 7
(C) 10
(D) 30

Question 185

A property owner who has a tenant needs to install a new roof. The total cost of the roof is $7,500. If the lifespan of the roof is 10 years, what is the yearly depreciation of the roof?

(A) $500
(B) $750
(C) $7,500
(D) The roof is determined a repair and cannot be depreciated

Question 186

The Town of Woodbridge has a millage rate of 26.5. Determine the amount of property tax for an assessed value of $220,000.

(A) $4,250
(B) $5,830
(C) $6,880
(D) $10,250

Question 187

What is not used as a comparative characteristic for a comparative market analysis (CMA)?

(A) Fireplaces
(B) Views
(C) Landscaping
(D) None of the above

Question 188

An investor decides to buy condominiums with five units for rent. The sales price of the condos was $600,000. What is the minimum average monthly rent per unit to yield a gross income multiplier of 5?

(A) $1,500
(B) $2,000
(C) $2,200
(D) $2,850

Question 189

What is the loss of value of a property due to factors that are external to the property?

(A) Deterioration
(B) Depreciation
(C) Functional obsolescence
(D) Economic obsolescence

Question 190

What method of the cost approach to appraisals includes construction costs based on a replica of the existing property?

(A) Capitalization
(B) Replacement
(C) Reproduction
(D) None of the above

Question 191

What work on a home can be classified as an repair and not a improvement?

(A) Bathroom renovation
(B) Addition of a deck
(C) Plumbing repair under a sink
(D) Installation of a security system

Question 192

What element of a valid contract ensures the presence of some exchange of value?

(A) Offer and acceptance
(B) Intention
(C) Consideration
(D) Legal capacity

Question 193

A dispute is taken to a court of law and it is determined that the contract is unenforceable. What is the consequence of the determination?

(A) The contract may still be executed
(B) The contract may still be executed except for the aspect in question
(C) The contract needs further review
(D) The contract is unenforceable and eliminates any obligations to both parties

Question 194

The legal removal of obligations from parties in a contract is:

(A) Breach of contract
(B) Recission
(C) Termination
(D) Compensation

Question 195

The statute of frauds requires which of the following stipulations?

(A) The contract must be in writing
(B) The contract must have a stipulated reasonable timeframe
(C) The contract must have an oral agreement
(D) The contract must include an exchange of value

Question 196

Up until what point is the providing of an earnest money deposit revokable?

(A) The check is written by the buyer
(B) The check is provided to the buyer's broker
(C) The broker communicates the acceptance of the offer to the seller
(D) The earnest money may be taken back at any time

Question 197

A buyer and seller have agreed to a purchase price. However, during the process, the buyer is not approved by the underwriter after a thorough review. What type of contingency would allow for the buyer to still receive their earnest money deposit back?

(A) Home sale
(B) Financing
(C) Kick-out clause
(D) Inspection

Question 198

A landlord with multiple properties hires a property manager. What type of client relationship is established?

(A) General
(B) Special
(C) Universal
(D) None of the above

Question 199

A prospective home buyer decides to let an uncle represent them as a real estate agent. They speak on the phone where the buyer expresses an intent to buy and then they discuss potential options. What agency creation method is established?

(A) Expressed
(B) Implied
(C) Necessity
(D) Contingent

Question 200

What is not one of the required legal responsibilities once agency is created?

(A) Loyalty
(B) Accounting
(C) Legal counsel
(D) Disclosure

Question 201

What is not one of the three options upon receipt of an offer?

(A) Acceptance
(B) Deference
(C) Rejection
(D) Counter

Question 202

A buyer and seller agree to a sales price of $250,000 on a primary residence. The buyer wishes to have the seller cover closing costs. If the buyer is putting down a 5% down payment, what is the maximum amount of seller concessions?

(A) $2,500
(B) $3,333
(C) $5,000
(D) $7,500

Question 203

A buyer and seller agree to seller financing. If the buyer of the property fails to meet the payments of the contract what recourse is available for the seller?

(A) The buyer must sell the property and provide proceeds to the seller
(B) The seller may evict the buyer as in a rental property
(C) The seller may foreclose and remove the buyer
(D) The seller has no recourse

Question 204

What is not one of the required elements of an option contract?

(A) Fixed price
(B) Premium
(C) Alternate
(D) Time frame

Question 205

Security deposits for a renter are kept:

(A) In an escrow account
(B) In a landlord's saving's account
(C) By the buyer's brokerage
(D) By the seller's brokerage

Question 206

What type of data below is excluded from being reported by a financial institution as a part of the Home Mortgage Disclosure Act?

(A) Data about ethnicity
(B) Loans on unimproved land
(C) The type of loan
(D) Loans for home improvement

Question 207

What HUD program provides law enforcement officers, teachers, firefighters, and emergency medical technicians with the opportunity to purchase homes located in revitalization areas at a discount?

(A) Rehabilitation Loan Mortgage Insurance
(B) Assisted Living Conversion Program
(C) Good Neighbor Next Door
(D) Self-Help Housing Property Disposition

Question 208

Which of the following is not an option for finding a HUD approved counselor?

(A) CFPB find a counselor tool
(B) Call HOPE 24/7 hotline
(C) Call HUD Hotline
(D) Call CFPB

Question 209

What is a true statement regarding a purchaser's ability to obtain a title report?

(A) The title report must be obtained from a lender recommended title company
(B) The title report must be obtained through an independent title company
(C) The title report must be obtained by the purchaser personally
(D) The title report may be obtained by the purchaser or through a title company

Question 210

What information is not published when a CFPB complaint is filed?

(A) Date of complaint
(B) Subject of complaint
(C) Description with consent
(D) Incurred penalty

Question 211

What Title of the Americans with Disabilities Act (ADA) requires that architectural and communication barriers are to be removed in existing facilities?

(A) I
(B) II
(C) III
(D) IV

Question 212

As per the Gramm-Leach Bliley Act, what is not a minimum requirement for a disclosure notice on the sharing of non-public information?

(A) How the information is used by affiliates
(B) With whom the information is shared
(C) Safeguards for the information
(D) What information is collected

Question 213

What is the latest permissible time for phone calls from telemarketers?

(A) 7 pm
(B) 8 pm
(C) 9 pm
(D) 10 pm

Question 214

Which of the following is not a factor when determining an individual's debt to income ratio?

(A) Student loans
(B) Gross income
(C) Net income
(D) Credit card payments

Question 215

If a borrower is delinquent on payments and the bank agrees to allow the borrower to sell the home for less than is owed, they are agreeing to which of the following?

(A) Forbearance
(B) Foreclosure
(C) Short Sale
(D) Avulsion

Question 216

As per the Equal Credit Opportunity Act (ECOA), it is permissible for an individual to be denied credit for which of the following reasons?

(A) Age
(B) Immigration status
(C) Gender
(D) Marital status

Question 217

Which of the following was enacted to prevent redlining?

(A) Bank Secrecy Act
(B) Truth in Lending Act
(C) Community Reinvestment Act
(D) US Patriot Act

Question 218

What scenario is least likely to be covered by general liability insurance for real estate professionals?

(A) Individual slips on ice during a showing
(B) A piece of personal property is broken during a showing
(C) A property is damaged during an inspection
(D) A company car is stolen

Question 219

A group of real estate brokers meet and decide to set the same price for commissions in a specific area. What prohibited practice is occurring?

(A) Price fixing
(B) Allocation of markets
(C) Tie-in agreement
(D) Group boycotting

Question 220

A homeowner allows the hazard insurance on the property to lapse. If the lender places insurance on the property without the consent of the borrower, it is called which of the following?

(A) Premium insurance
(B) Title insurance
(C) Force-placed insurance
(D) Mortgage insurance

Question 221

What environmental protection act regulates the discharge of pollutants into bodies of water?

(A) Resource Recovery Act
(B) Clean Water Act
(C) The Comprehensive Environmental Response, Compensation, and Liability Act
(D) Flood Control Act

Question 222

A property built before what year is subject to concerns related to lead-based paint?

(A) 1955
(B) 1960
(C) 1970
(D) 1978

Question 223

A property for sale is known to have contamination levels in the ground. What environmental site assessment phase is appropriate for the site?

(A) I
(B) II
(C) III
(D) IV

Question 224

What known hazardous substance does not have a significant potential risk to an individual's respiratory health?

(A) Asbestos
(B) Radon
(C) Mold
(D) None of the above

Question 225

What designated flood zone is considered a high-risk area?

(A) Zone A
(B) Zone B
(C) Zone D
(D) Zone X

Question 226

The act of encouraging repeated refinancing of a loan without any real benefit to the borrower is which of the following practices?

(A) Redlining
(B) Steering
(C) Loan Flipping
(D) Ballooning

Question 227

Which of the following loan types are subject to up-front mortgage insurance premiums?

(A) Conventional loan with 20% down
(B) VA loan with 10% down
(C) Conventional loan with 10% down
(D) FHA loan with 20% down

Question 228

Which of the following loan types require two sets of fees to be applied at closing?

(A) Construction-to-permanent loan
(B) Jumbo loan
(C) Balloon loan
(D) Construction only loan

Question 229

Which of the following fees are not allowed for a VA loan?

(A) Discount points
(B) Attorney fees charged by a lender
(C) Lender fee
(D) Title insurance

Question 230

A borrower wishes to refinance an existing loan to remove the PMI from the monthly payment. How long after the first payment must she wait to be able to eliminate PMI?

(A) 1 year
(B) 2 years
(C) 5 years
(D) 10 years

Question 231

According to the TILA-RESPA integrated disclosures, all of the following must be included in the loan estimate to consider it received except:

(A) Property sale history
(B) Consumer name
(C) Consumer income
(D) Property address

Question 232

If a recording fee decreases from the loan estimate to the closing disclosure, which of the following statements are true?

(A) The fee is not included in the cumulation of fees
(B) The fee is included in the cumulation of fees
(C) The fee is not included in the cumulation of fees for the zero-tolerance requirement
(D) The fee is included in the cumulation of fees for the zero-tolerance requirement only

Question 233

How long after consummation may a revised closing disclosure be provided?

(A) 15 business days
(B) 15 calendar days
(C) 30 calendar days
(D) 30 business days

Question 234

A proposed loan amount of $300,000 will have an interest rate of 4.25%. However, the borrower chooses to buy 2 points on the loan for a lower interest rate. Considering only the loan amount and the points, what is the new amount to be financed?

(A) $300,600
(B) $306,000
(C) $360,000
(D) $294,000

Question 235

An investor decides to purchase real estate as a vacation rental. The original purchase price is $350,000 and additionally an extra $10,000 in remodeling costs. The property is kept for five years with an accumulation of $5,000 per year in rental income. If the property is sold for a net profit of $20,000 at the end of five years, what is the return on investment?

(A) 12.5%
(B) 20%
(C) 33%
(D) 120%

Question 236

Using an estimated annual rate of 3%, what is the appreciated home value for a property sold for $200,000 after five years?

(A) $215,200
(B) $222,860
(C) $231,855
(D) $245,890

Question 237

A single tax filer sells a home for $350,000. If the closing costs are estimated at 5%, what is the minimum existing mortgage payoff amount in which the seller is exempt from capital gain taxes?

(A) $82,500
(B) $100,000
(C) $112,500
(D) $120,000

Question 238

A buyer who is agrees to a purchase price of $200,000. What is the minimum amount of down payment to avoid PMI on a conventional loan?

(A) $10,000
(B) $20,000
(C) $30,000
(D) $40,000

Question 239

Calculate the per diem interest over a 30-day period if a loan has a balance of $242,000 and an interest rate of 4.25%.

(A) $34.25
(B) $710.22
(C) $744.23
(D) $845.34

Question 240

A fixed-rate mortgage has a P & I monthly payment of $820. The yearly tax bill is $6000 and the Hazard Insurance is $1200 per year. If the loan includes a PMI of $82 per month, what is the total monthly payment of the loan?

(A) $1288
(B) $1502
(C) $1625
(D) $1822

Solution 1

Since the property is to be repurposed for condominiums, it can now be classified as residential.

The answer is **(A)**

Solution 2

The plant as a house plant is easily movable and can be considered a chattel. Once the plant becomes attached to the land, it now is real property.

The answer is **(A)**

Solution 3

Trade fixtures are pieces of property that a tenant affixes to a leased building or land for the purpose of conducting business. This would include a cooktop or other equipment attached to the property as long as they are still removable.

The answer is **(C)**

Solution 4

Land characteristics can be classified as either economic or physical. Land has three distinct physical characteristics:

- Immobility
- Indestructibility
- Uniqueness

The answer is **(B)**

Solution 5

A property must be fully enclosed. To do this the point of beginning (POB) must be met by the point of ending (POE).

The answer is **(C)**

Solution 6

The lot-and-block system identifies plots of land by a lot number or letter and the block in which the lot is located. However, the block itself is located by using either the metes-and-bounds system or the rectangular survey system.

The answer is **(C)**

Solution 7

A property survey confirms or determines a property's boundary lines and the specifics of any other restrictions for the property. A survey can determine the following information for a property:

- Legal boundaries
- Easements
- Elevation
- Hazard Areas

The answer is **(B)**

Solution 8

An encroachment is when a property owner violates the established property rights agreed to with the neighbors. The fence being built on a neighbor's property without an agreement would be an encroachment.

The answer is **(A)**

Solution 9

Covenants, conditions, and restrictions (CC&Rs) are the established rules for a home AS a part of a homeowners' association (HOA). They establish rules and limitations on living in the community.

The answer is **(C)**

Solution 10

Police power gives the government the right to enact regulations for the health, safety, and welfare of the public. Some examples that fall under this category include:

- Building codes
- Zoning laws

- Safety regulations
- Rights of tenants and landlords
- Environmental regulations and control
- Right to damage property for the best public interest

The answer is **(A)**

Solution 11

Tenants by entirety allows for the passing of property at death to not require any legal process or documents. This is due to the fact that this type of ownership sees the married couple as a single entity.

The answer is **(C)**

Solution 12

Fee Simple Determinable includes an interest in property that is terminated automatically upon the occurrence or non-occurrence of an event or condition.

The answer is **(B)**

Solution 13

A bundle of rights is the set of legal privileges that is generally afforded to a real estate buyer with the transfer of the title. The bundle includes the following:

- The right of possession
- The right of control
- The right of exclusion
- The right of enjoyment
- The right of disposition

The answer is **(D)**

Solution 14

Estate at will is where a tenant occupies a property with the consent of the owner but without a formal written contract or lease.

The answer is **(C)**

Solution 15

Estate at sufferance is an agreement in which a tenant is legally permitted to live on a property after a lease term has expired but before the landlord has provided notice to vacate

The answer is **(B)**

Solution 16

In a net lease, the tenant is responsible for some or all costs associated such as utilities, maintenance, insurance, and others. The net agreement can be single, double, or triple which indicates the number of responsibilities beyond the required rent. Therefore, a double net lease would include rent plus property taxes and insurance.

The answer is **(C)**

Solution 17

A percentage lease is an agreement with commercial tenants in which there is a requirement to pay the landlord a fixed percentage of gross revenue earned from business conducted at the property. In this scenario, the agreed percentage is 10%. Therefore, with a gross revenue of $5,000, the tenant owes the landlord rent plus an additional $500 which is 10% of $5,000. The total payment is $800 + $500 = $1,300.

The answer is **(B)**

Solution 18

If there are multiple loans on a single property, there is an established hierarchy that dictates which loans get paid first by remaining assets in the event of failure to pay. In this case, the first mortgage has seniority and the second mortgage is a junior lien. Therefore, the first mortgage gets paid by the proceeds from the sale and anything remaining gets applied to the second mortgage. Once the $150,000 is paid off, there is $20,000 remaining and the second mortgage balance is reduced to $40,000.

The answer is **(C)**

Solution 19

A gift deed is used for the transfer of real estate between relatives where no exchange of money has taken place.

The answer is **(B)**

Solution 20

Adverse possession is when an individual other than the owner uses a piece of property openly, publicly, and without the owner's consent for a specified period of time. If an individual wishes to successfully claim adverse possession they must exhibit the following:

- Continuous use
- Hostile takeover
- Open and notorious possession
- Actual possession
- Exclusive use

The answer is **(D)**

Solution 21

Implied actual notice is when an individual witnesses something that provided them with information about the property. No one has told the individual directly nor is there written evidence of the information being conveyed but it is reasonable to assume that the information or event provided the necessary notice.

The answer is **(B)**

Solution 22

Utility is a measure of the usefulness of a property. Each individual buyer has a minimum level of utility such as no less than three bedrooms, be near the ocean, or other specific features. In this scenario the home's utility must satisfy the need for five bedrooms.

The answer is **(B)**

Solution 23

The income approach is used to estimate the value of income-producing properties.

The answer is **(B)**

Solution 24

Choosing comparable properties does not have exact requirements but should be as close as possible in size, location, age, and other characteristics. The comparable homes should also be sold as recently as possible. Of the options listed, an age difference of 35 years is a noticeable gap and should not be used as a comparable based on the information provided.

The answer is **(C)**

Solution 25

It is acceptable for a consumer to obtain multiple appraisals

The answer is **(C)**

Solution 26

Properties are depreciated over a period of 27.5 years.

The answer is **(C)**

Solution 27

Since the property taxes are based on assessed value and not market value, the price needs to be converted using the assessment ratio:

$$Assessed\ Value = \$200,000\ x\ 0.8 = \$160,000$$

Then, to determine the property taxes, multiply the assessed value by the millage rate and divide by $1,000:

$$Property\ Tax = \frac{\$160,000\ x\ 14.8}{\$1,000} = \$2,368$$

The answer is **(A)**

Solution 28

To get the value of the home, first get the average of the adjusted prices per square foot:

$$Average = \frac{\$200 + \$180 + \$175}{3} = \$185$$

Then multiply this average by the square feet of the subject property to find its CMA value:

$$CMA\ Value = \$185\ x\ 2000 = \$370,000$$

The answer is **(C)**

Solution 29

Using the comparable property, we can determine the gross income multiplier:

$$Gross\ Income\ Multiplier = \frac{Sale\ Price}{Gross\ Annual\ Rental\ Income} = \frac{\$280,000}{\$30,000} = 9.33$$

Then we can use this multiplier to determine the estimated value of the property for sale:

$$Estimate\ Value = Gross\ Income\ Multiplier\ x\ Gross\ Annual\ Rent$$
$$= 9.33\ x\ \$24,000 = \$224,000$$

The answer is **(A)**

Solution 30

Functional obsolescence is the reduction of a home's value due to outdated features that cannot be easily changed.

The answer is **(C)**

Solution 31

The cost approach is appropriate when the consideration of construction is a factor. Some of the most common examples include:

- New homes
- Insurance coverage
- Commercial properties

Rental properties are better suited for the income approach which factors in the amount of income the owner can expect from the properties.

The answer is **(D)**

Solution 32

To determine value as per the cost approach, the property's value is determined by the cost of land, plus total costs of construction, less depreciation:

$$Property\ Value = Cost\ of\ Construction + Cost\ of\ Land - Depreciation$$

Therefore, the property value is:

$$\$150,000 + \$45,000 - \$5,000 = \$190,000$$

The answer is **(C)**

Solution 33

Once an express contract has been established and agreed upon, an identical implied contract cannot exist.

The answer is **(C)**

Solution 34

A bilateral contract is one in which each party promises to perform an act in exchange for the other party's promise to perform. This is the typical type of real estate sales contract.

The answer is **(B)**

Solution 35

An unenforceable contract will not hold up in a court of law and eliminates any obligations imposed on parties in the contract. A contract can be considered unenforceable if the elements of a valid contract are not met. This includes errors in the contract.

The answer is **(D)**

Solution 36

Termination is the ending of a contract before all obligations are met to fully execute the contract. Termination for cause is when a material breach of contract occurs.

The answer is **(A)**

Solution 37

The sale of a property gives the new owner an interest in the property called the equitable title.

The answer is **(A)**

Solution 38

Inspection contingencies stipulate a cost of repairs that if exceeded, allows the buyer to be relieved of the contractual obligations and receive their earnest money back in full. The amount is often specified as a percentage of the sales price. In this case, 2% of $200,000 is $4,000.

The answer is **(B)**

Solution 39

The agent has certain legal obligations and responsibilities to the client once the agreement is established. Among those includes obedience which is a requirement for the agent to promptly and completely follow any instructions from the client as long as they are lawful in nature.

The answer is **(C)**

Solution 40

Time is of the essence is a legal phrase that when used in a contract enforces parties to act in a reasonable or specified timeframe.

The answer is **(C)**

Solution 41

A negotiation between a buyer and a seller may include additional items other than the purchase price. Some of those may include:

- Closing cost share
- Earnest money deposit amount
- Closing date

- Contract contingencies

The answer is **(D)**

Solution 42

For any FHA loan, the seller concessions are capped at 6%.

The answer is **(C)**

Solution 43

An installment sales contract is an agreement where a buyer of real estate agrees to pay the seller the full amount of the purchase price broken up in installments over time. This may allow the seller to be able to reduce capital gains taxes by spreading out the gain over a period of time.

The answer is **(B)**

Solution 44

An options contract is an agreement between two parties to facilitate a potential transaction involving an asset at a preset price and date. The buyer gets the exclusive right to buy the property but is not obligated to do so upon the time the option is available.

The answer is **(C)**

Solution 45

In a net listing agreement, the commission is based on the difference between the established baseline price and the actual sales price. Therefore, the commission is $170,000 - $150,000 = $20,000.

The answer is **(C)**

Solution 46

An open listing allows the owner to place listings with multiple real estate brokers. This listing type is not included in MLS.

The answer is **(C)**

Solution 47

The specific exemptions to the Fair Housing Act are:

- Rental of a room in a dwelling with no more than four independent units
- Housing operated by private organizations or clubs which restrict membership
- Single-family purchase without a mortgage broker

The answer is **(D)**

Solution 48

When a professional takes advantage of an ill-informed borrower for personal gain, this is called predatory lending.

The answer is **(A)**

Solution 49

Title I of the ADA applies to employment. Qualified persons with a disability who can perform the essential functions of the job with or without reasonable accommodation must not be discriminated against in job application procedures, hiring, firing, advancement, compensation, job training, and other terms, conditions, and privileges of employment.

The answer is **(A)**

Solution 50

The Multiple listing service is a database for the sharing and exchange of information between real estate professionals. It is divided regionally and professionals can become members of more than one region if needed.

The answer is **(A)**

Solution 51

Information is publicly available if an institution has a reasonable basis to believe that the information is lawfully available to the general public. A phone book fits this description.

The answer is **(A)**

Solution 52

The identified risk for the buyer is the concern that if the property is purchased, the roof will need to be replaced or cause additional damage to the home. By proposing to share the costs, the buyer's mitigation strategy is transference which is the sharing or transferring of the risk to another party.

The answer is **(C)**

Solution 53

When an attractive product is presented to get a potential customer engaged but then is sold a different product, this is a bait and switch.

The answer is **(C)**

Solution 54

Tie-in agreements are an agreement to sell one product but only with the condition that the buyer also purchases a different product or service.

The answer is **(D)**

Solution 55

A title search can return a number of issues that may not be readily apparent. Among them are liens, encumbrance, forgeries, boundary disputes, and others. If there is an agreement to access the land, this is called an easement.

The answer is **(C)**

Solution 56

There are three rules as established by the Gramm-Leach Bliley Act:

- The Financial Privacy Rule: requires providing customers with privacy disclosure
- Safeguard Rule: Requires written security plans by institutions
- Pretexting Prohibition: Prohibits the practice of collecting information under false pretenses

The answer is **(A)**

Solution 57

TILA section 1026.36(e) covers the prohibition of steering a consumer towards a specific loan type or transaction. The consumer must be presented with the loan options in section 3 which include:

- The loan with the lowest interest rate;
- The loan with the lowest interest rate without negative amortization, a prepayment penalty, interest-only payments, a balloon payment in the first 7 years of the life of the loan, a demand feature, shared equity, or shared appreciation; or, in the case of a reverse mortgage, a loan without a prepayment penalty, or shared equity or shared appreciation; and
- The loan with the lowest total dollar amount of discount points, origination points, or origination fees (or, if two or more loans have the same total dollar amount of discount points, origination points, or origination fees, the loan with the lowest interest rate that has the lowest total dollar amount of discount points, origination points or origination fees).

While origination fees are a part of option "C" a loan with solely the lowest origination fees is not required.

The answer is **(D)**

Solution 58

While property management companies are responsible for facilitating maintenance requests, they most often do not perform the maintenance themselves. They will hire licensed contractors to perform the repairs necessary.

The answer is **(D)**

Solution 59

If a property that was previously in a moderate-risk flood area moves to a high-risk area, FEMA now requires flood insurance and will notify the property owner.

The answer is **(A)**

Solution 60

Errors and omissions insurance (E&O) is malpractice insurance coverage for real estate professionals to pay for claims related to error, omission, or negligence in an agent's duties.

Common exclusions include claims resulting from dishonest or criminal acts, if the agent caused bodily harm or death to another person, or if there is damage to someone's property.

The answer is **(A)**

Solution 61

Brownfields contain or may contain hazardous materials. They may be revitalized but are most often undertaken by state programs and are not under Federal oversight. Superfunds are hazardous sites that are Federally handled.

The answer is **(D)**

Solution 62

Disclosure requirements vary by state and may be different. Some only require the structure condition and others include the land as well.

The answer is **(B)**

Solution 63

The Superfund Amendments and Reauthorization Act amended the Comprehensive Environmental Response, Compensation, and Liability Act. The changes to the Act include:

- Stressed the importance of permanent remedies and innovative treatment technologies in cleaning up hazardous waste sites
- Required Superfund actions to consider the standards and requirements found in other State and Federal environmental laws and regulations
- Provided new enforcement authorities and settlement tools
- Increased State involvement
- Increased the focus on human health problems posed by hazardous waste sites
- Encouraged greater citizen participation in making decisions on how sites should be cleaned up
- Increased the size of the trust fund to $8.5 billion.
- Revised the Hazard Ranking System

The answer is **(A)**

Solution 64

Asbestos was banned as a construction material in 1978. Therefore, any home transaction involving a property that was built before 1978 may include this hazardous material.

The answer is **(C)**

Solution 65

A Phase II environmental assessment is used to determine whether contamination is in fact present. This would include activities such as sampling and other physical tests.

The answer is **(B)**

Solution 66

The CFPB has a number of functions related to consumer protection. They do not dictate the actions of consumers.

The answer is **(D)**

Solution 67

The VA loan allows the borrower to put down no money.

The answer is **(B)**

Solution 68

The secondary mortgage market is where mortgages are bought and sold as securities. An aggregator is an entity that purchases mortgages from financial institutions and then securitizes them into mortgage-backed securities (MBS).

The answer is **(D)**

Solution 69

FHA sets limits on the amount that can be borrowed. It is dependent on the geographical area in which the loan is taken and the median sale price in that area. However, it can never be higher than the ceiling or lower than the floor in any area. If the county is determined to be in the lowest cost market, this means that the floor will apply.

The answer is **(A)**

Solution 70

While a down payment of 20% can avoid the need for PMI and a borrower can apply to have PMI removed at 80% LTV, it will automatically stop at 78%.

The answer is **(B)**

Solution 71

TILA section 1026.24(i) provides prohibited acts in advertising. In this situation, we are directed specifically to section 1026.24(i)(1)(ii) which discusses non-variable-rate transactions and the term fixed. The requirement is that any use of the term "fixed" shall be accompanied by the time period for which the rate or payment is fixed and the fact that the rate may vary.

The answer is **(D)**

Solution 72

There are 3 types of tolerance thresholds:

- Zero tolerance: As the name implies there may be no increase from estimate to closing disclosure
- 10% cumulative tolerance: The change in all fees must not be more than 10%
- No or unlimited tolerance: Any change is acceptable

The answer is **(A)**

Solution 73

The loan estimate expires 10 days after issuing.

The answer is **(A)**

Solution 74

The HELOC is a way for a borrower to tap into the equity of an existing home loan for other purposes. To calculate, the borrower is only allowed to have a total owed amount of 90% of the value of the home: 0.90 X 450,000 = $405,000. Then subtract what is already owed: 405,000 − 300,000 = $105,000

The answer is **(C)**

Solution 75

A simple-interest loan calculates interest on a daily basis as opposed to monthly like a traditional loan. To calculate, divide the rate by 365 days and multiply by the outstanding balance and then multiply by the number of days in the period:

$$Interest = \left(\frac{0.04}{365}\right)(100,000)(30) = \$328.77$$

The answer is **(B)**

Solution 76

The estimated cash to close is the sum of the cost minus any previous deposits or seller credits. In this case: 8200 + 19500 − 5000 = $22700.

The answer is **(C)**

Solution 77

Points are used to lower interest rates and each point will lower the rate by 0.25%.

The answer is **(A)**

Solution 78

The new adjustable rate is the index plus the margin: 3 + 2.5 = 5.5%. The new rate is now 0.5% higher than the previous loan. To find the increase, divide the interest rate by the number of months and multiply by the balance:

$$Monthly\ Interest\ Increase = \frac{0.005}{12} x\ 158000 = \$65.83$$

The answer is **(A)**

Solution 79

The prepaid section includes insurance, MIP, prepaid interest, and property taxes. In this scenario:

Taxes = (5000)/12 x 3 = 1250
Insurance = 1100/2 = 550
Interest = 17.25 x 10 = 172.50

Sum = $1972

The answer is **(A)**

Solution 80

The combined LTV is simply a ratio of the addition of the loans to the addition of the values. In this case, we want the overall LTV to be at least 80% so the equation becomes:

$$0.80 = \frac{Loan\ 1 + Loan\ 2}{Value\ 1 + Value\ 2} = \frac{230000 + Loan\ 2}{280000 + 220000}; Loan\ 2 = \$170,000$$

The down payment is then $220,000 - $170,000 = $50,000

The percent is 50000/220000 = 22.7%

The answer is **(D)**

Solution 81

Special purpose property is used by and for the public. This may include cemeteries, government buildings, libraries, parks, places of worship, and schools.

The answer is **(D)**

Solution 82

The classification of a fixture is a chattel that becomes attached to the land. The classification can be based on whether or not the item can be easily moved. A furnace is not a permanent part of the home but is not easily moved and becomes a fixture of the home.

The answer is **(A)**

Solution 83

The criteria used to classify whether property is a fixture or not includes:

- How is the item attached?
- Inclusion of the item with the construction of the property.
- Agreement between the buyer and seller.

The value of the property of inconsequential.

The answer is **(A)**

Solution 84

The elements of a bill of sale include:

- Date of purchase
- Name and address of the seller and buyer
- Amount paid for the transfer of ownership
- Description of the assets being transferred
- Guarantee that the item is free from all claims and offsets
- Representations or warranties
- Signatures of the seller, of the buyer, and a notary public

The answer is **(D)**

Solution 85

Permanence of investment is an economic characteristic that indicates that a portion of work performed on the land is considered to have permanent value. Not all improvements retain value but some that have permanence include items such as drainage, electricity, water, and sewer systems.

The answer is **(C)**

Solution 86

There are 3 methods used to determine the exact location and boundaries of a parcel of land:

- Metes-and-bounds
- Rectangular survey
- Lot-and-block

The answer is **(A)**

Solution 87

The metes-and-bounds method establishes a point of beginning (POB) from a monument or landmark. Metes, which are boundary lines that enclose the bounds, are then established between points until the point of ending is reached.

The answer is **(B)**

Solution 88

CC&R's dictate the rules for a community by an HOA. They may have limitations or restrictions related to how the owner may use or modify the property.

The answer is **(D)**

Solution 89

Compensation for eminent domain must be provided and the value shall be fair market value.

The answer is **(C)**

Solution 90

Escheat is the ability of the government to obtain properties that are unclaimed. This most commonly occurs when there is no clear heir and an owner has died.

The answer is **(D)**

Solution 91

A homeowner who does not agree with the action of eminent domain imposed on them may challenge the decision in a court of law. They may seek legal counsel and an appraisal to ensure proper treatment. They shall not destroy or no longer maintain the property and still expect proper value.

The answer is **(D)**

Solution 92

Tenancy in common is a type of ownership where two or more persons hold title to real estate jointly with equal or unequal percentages of ownership.

The answer is **(B)**

Solution 93

Fee Simple Subject to a Condition Subsequent allows for an interest that can be terminated at the will of a future interest holder upon the occurrence or non-occurrence of an event or condition.

The answer is **(C)**

Solution 94

The right of possession upon transfer of title identifies the titleholder as the legal owner of the property.

The answer is **(A)**

Solution 95

In a life estate, the life tenant cannot sell the property unless the remainderman provides written consent to do so.

The answer is **(D)**

Solution 96

Despite the lack of a written agreement, an estate at will still has certain legal obligations that must be met by both the tenant and the landlord. Subject to state law, both must give notice to the other property of intent to vacate the property and typically this shall be at least a 30-day notice.

The answer is **(D)**

Solution 97

For a triple lease agreement, the tenant is responsible for the rent plus all additional expenses incurred. Therefore, the total payment of the tenant is the sum of all costs: $900 + $300 + $90 + $150 = $1,440.

The answer is **(D)**

Solution 98

The hierarchy of loans establishes the payment to lien holders from proceeds if there is a failure of payment. The proceeds will go to the highest priority loan first until it is fully satisfied and then on to the next until all proceeds are exhausted. This may result in some creditors receiving zero in payment.

The answer is **(D)**

Solution 99

The property owner generally has exclusive rights to the soil, minerals, and any other materials found underneath the land. If there are any deviations to this, it must be disclosed in the title deed at the time of purchase. If no restrictions are indicated, it can be assumed the buyer has full subsurface rights to the property unless this is not stipulated under state law.

The answer is **(A)**

Solution 100

A special or limited warranty deed stipulates that the grantor only warrants any title defect from the time the grantor took possession of the property, but not prior.

The answer is **(B)**

Solution 101

Constructive notice is information that is printed in the public record. This is sufficient to assume that an individual should be aware if needed regardless of formal acknowledgment.

The answer is **(C)**

Solution 102

The chain of title traces the historical transfer of ownership from the current owner back to the original owner. The chain of title is much more detailed in the specifics of ownership than the abstract of title.

The answer is **(B)**

Solution 103

Purchasing power is the ability of a buyer to afford the home. The more people that can afford the property, the more available buyers. Sometimes, in scenarios of very high-priced homes, the potential pool of buyers can be limited and the price may have to go down to attract additional suitors.

The answer is **(C)**

Solution 104

For a building that is not frequently sold, the cost approach determines what the value of the property may be by assuming a reasonable buyer would not pay more than a comparable building on a comparable lot. Often this is most appropriate for buildings such as schools, hospitals, or government buildings that are not bought and sold frequently.

The answer is **(C)**

Solution 105

Just because a document or source discusses a property's value does not mean it can be used as a valuation. This is certainly true for public information.

The answer is **(D)**

Solution 106

An appraiser must not be influenced in any way to make a decision. They may, however, be alerted to additional information.

The answer is **(C)**

Solution 107

A broker price opinion (BPO) is an unofficial assessment of a property's potential market value based on expert judgment. A BPO is often based on qualitative and subjective factors such as neighborhood characteristics, curb appeal, and current market trends. A broker price opinion costs much less and can be done more quickly than an official appraisal of the property.

The answer is **(D)**

Solution 108

The difference in the living area is 1,800 – 1,500 = 300 sq. ft. Therefore, the total adjustment is:

$$Adjustment = \left(\frac{300}{100}\right) x\ \$1{,}000 = \$3{,}000$$

Then since the home in question has the greater amount of square feet, the adjustment is made to increase the value of the comparable and the adjustment is positive.

The answer is **(D)**

Solution 109

A gross income multiplier is an estimate of the value of an investment property. It is typically calculated by dividing the property's sale price by its estimated or provided gross annual rental income.

The answer is **(B)**

Solution 110

The replacement method determines the cost of a new structure with newer materials, current construction methods, and design.

The answer is **(B)**

Solution 111

A valid contract shall contain the following elements:

- Offer and acceptance
- Intention
- Consideration
- Legal capacity
- Legality

The answer is **(C)**

Solution 112

While a void contract is often considered not executable by design, a contract may be deemed voidable if the agreement is actionable, but the circumstances surrounding the agreement are questionable in nature. This includes agreements made where one party withheld information or intentionally provided inaccurate information.

The answer is **(C)**

Solution 113

A minor breach of contract is the deliverable of the contract by the other party, but the party failed to fulfill some part of their obligation. The missing of a deadline but still providing the deliverable qualifies as a minor breach.

The answer is **(B)**

Solution 114

Punitive damages are legal payments that are imposed on a defendant found guilty.

The answer is **(B)**

Solution 115

Liquidated damages cover losses in the event of a breach of contract by the other in which the monetary damages would be difficult to determine.

The answer is **(A)**

Solution 116

The actual breach of contract has not occurred yet, but there is information to indicate that the other party in the agreement will be in breach if the action is completed. This is anticipatory breach.

The answer is **(C)**

Solution 117

Recission is the legal removal of obligations from parties in a contract. The court determines that the parties shall be returned to the point of obligation as if the contract was never executed.

The answer is **(D)**

Solution 118

A kick-out clause allows the seller to accept an offer from another qualified buyer. However, the seller must give the current buyer a specified amount of time to match the qualifications of the new buyer. Otherwise, the seller can back out of the contract and sell to the new buyer.

The answer is **(B)**

Solution 119

A special agent relationship is the representation of an individual for a specific singular task or transaction.

The answer is **(C)**

Solution 120

The recognition of legal agency varies by state law and some do require a written agreement for it to hold up but some find implied agency acceptable.

The answer is **(C)**

Solution 121

A counteroffer voids a previous offer and the entity that presented that offer is no longer legally responsible for it.

The answer is **(D)**

Solution 122

The buyer may negotiate for the seller to cover closing costs. But these amounts are limited based on the loan type and the down payment amount.

The answer is **(A)**

Solution 123

For loans that are seller-financed, the agreement allows the buyer and seller to agree on the terms of the payments including the interest rate.

The answer is **(D)**

Solution 124

An option contract will set a predetermined specific price that the buyer may choose to agree to within the timeframe and stipulations of the contract.

The answer is **(A)**

Solution 125

Legal advice and counsel do not fall under the expertise of a real estate professional and shall not be provided.

The answer is **(B)**

Solution 126

An exclusive agency listing is an agreement between a seller and brokerage for exclusive rights for the sale of a home. In this type of agreement, the seller retains the right to market and sell the home to a buyer without having to pay a commission.

The answer is **(C)**

Solution 127

The security deposit covers the landlord in the event of damage or failure to pay by the tenant. Improvements to the home are not necessitated from failure of the tenant to fulfill obligations and therefore use of the deposit to cover these costs would be unlawful.

The answer is **(D)**

Solution 128

The Fair Housing Act requires advertisements to make the consumer aware of the seller's participation in the requirements of equal housing lending. They do not need to go into detail about what the Act requires in ads.

The answer is **(A)**

Solution 129

Steering is forcing a specific geographical area on an applicant based on race, religion, or ethnicity and it is strictly prohibited.

The answer is **(A)**

Solution 130

A multiple listing service (MLS) is a private database created, maintained and paid for by real estate professionals to help their clients buy and sell property. Home sellers can't post their home directly to the MLS, because access to this database is limited to licensed agents and brokers who pay for membership. Each regional MLS has its own listings and clients may become a member of more than one.

The answer is **(C)**

Solution 131

Discrimination is prohibited as a part of:

- Fair Housing Act
- Civil Rights Act
- Home Mortgage Disclosure Act
- The Community Reinvestment Act

The answer is **(D)**

Solution 132

As per ADA Title III, if a real estate broker or salesperson has a home office in which business is conducted with customers, that portion of the home must also be in compliance with the ADA.

The answer is **(B)**

Solution 133

The ability to opt-out must be provided along with a reasonable time frame but the third party for which information will be provided does not have to be identified.

The answer is **(C)**

Solution 134

If a real estate sales office has 15 or more employees, they are subject to Title I.

The answer is **(D)**

Solution 135

Subprime mortgages are less qualified borrowers. A DTI of 40% while not great is not considered an issue usually. More often it will be closer to or above 50% to be considered subprime.

The answer is **(B)**

Solution 136

FHA requires 3 months before the resale of a home.

The answer is **(A)**

Solution 137

Risks are not necessarily a detrimental factor as they can be identified as either a threat or an opportunity.

The answer is **(C)**

Solution 138

Vicarious liability is a situation in which one party is held partly responsible for the unlawful actions of a third party. This can occur in real estate between a broker and an agent even if the broker is unaware of the actions of the agent.

The answer is **(B)**

Solution 139

FEMA requirements stipulate that the flood coverage must be at least the lesser of:

1. The maximum amount of NFIP coverage available for the particular property type, or
2. The outstanding principal balance of the loan, or
3. The insurable value of the structure.

The answer is **(B)**

Solution 140

The allocation of markets or customers is the agreement to divide areas with customers so that there is no competition within markets.

The answer is **(C)**

Solution 141

By EPA definition, an underground storage tank (UST) is defined as "a tank and any underground piping connected to the tank that has at least 10 percent of its combined volume underground."

The answer is **(A)**

Solution 142

Mold is organic growth in areas of high moisture. Mold is common in areas of the home such as around leaks in roofs, windows, or pipes, or where there has been flooding.

The answer is **(C)**

Solution 143

A Phase I primarily assesses the likelihood that a site is contaminated through visual observations, historical use reviews, and regulatory records.

The answer is **(A)**

Solution 144

The acceptable limit is determined on the state level but the generally accepted action level established by the World Health Organization is 2.7 pCi/L.

The answer is **(B)**

Solution 145

Section 10 of RESPA stipulates that the lender may require a cushion for an escrow account no more than 1/6 of the total yearly disbursements.

The answer is **(B)**

Solution 146

Section 1002.6(b)(5) provides guidance on what income to be considered as a part of the applicant's creditworthiness. The creditor must include all sources of income including part-time wages, pensions, alimony, etc. but does have the ability to evaluate the inclusion of income on the basis of its likelihood to continue.

The answer is **(C)**

Solution 147

The FHA loan is the only which is 100% backed. The VA and USDA are partially and conventional is 0%.

The answer is **(B)**

Solution 148

A balloon payment does not fully amortize over the life of the loan and there is a remaining balance at the end of the term. The advantage can be that the monthly payments and the rates are less. This lends itself to be advantageous in the short term and not the long term. Therefore, if someone were to be sure they are selling in a short period of time, the balloon mortgage may make sense.

The answer is **(B)**

Solution 149

An FHA loan has a minimum down payment of 3.5% but the credit score of the individual must be at least 580. If it drops to between 500 and 580, the minimum is 10%.

The answer is **(C)**

Solution 150

FHA maximum debt ratios are 31 on the front end and 43 on the back end.

The answer is **(B)**

Solution 151

The ECOA requires the lender or mortgage broker to consider reliable sources of income such as part-time, pensions, alimony, social security, public assistance, and others. However, the applicant is not required to submit alimony, child support, or separate maintenance as income.

The answer is **(A)**

Solution 152

PMI is used as protection for the lender. The borrower is in no way protected if there is a failure to pay the monthly payments.

The answer is **(A)**

Solution 153

TRID stipulates that the lender must deliver the application no later than 3 business days after application.

The answer is **(A)**

Solution 154

The TIP is the ratio of the total amount of interest paid to the total loan amount:

$$TIP = \left(\frac{100}{200}\right) x\ 100 = 50\%$$

The answer is **(B)**

Solution 155

For a principal residence or secondary home purchase, the limit on seller concessions is limited depending on the amount of the down payment. For an investment property, however, the down payment does not matter and it is a consistent 2%.

The answer is **(A)**

Solution 156

Commission is based on the sales price of the home. It is common for the two agents to split the commission and to be paid by the seller. To determine the commission:

$$Commission = Sales\ Price\ X\ Commission\ Rate = \$350,000\ x\ 0.03 = \$10,500$$

The answer is **(B)**

Solution 157

A prepayment penalty is capped at 2% for the first two years and 1% thereafter.

The answer is **(B)**

Solution 158

Debt-to-income (DTI) ratio is a comparison of a borrower's income to obligations. In this case, we know the target ratio and we have to back figure the maximum mortgage:

$$DTI = \frac{(Mortgage + Debt\ Payments)}{Monthly\ Income} = 0.40 = \frac{(Mortgage + 800)}{5750}; Mortgage = \$1500$$

The answer is **(B)**

Solution 159

For the 10% cumulative rule all of the fees combined must not increase by more than 10%: 5000 x 1.1 = $5500.

The answer is **(B)**

Solution 160

The housing ratio, also known as the front-end ratio, is the housing payment divided by the monthly income. The monthly income is 60000/12 = 5000. The equation becomes:

$$0.28 = \left(\frac{450 + 90 + 120 + Mortgage\ Payment}{5000}\right)$$

If you solve for the mortgage payment you get $740.

The answer is **(A)**

Solution 161

Real property is land or things attached to land which cannot be moved. Trees or plants that grow on land can also be considered real property. The exception is those that require routine cultivation or labor, such as crops.

The answer is **(C)**

Solution 162

Chattels are tangible personal property such as furniture or clothing. Additionally, some chattels can be attached to land and become part of real property. Patents are intangible property and are not chattels.

The answer is **(D)**

Solution 163

The trade fixtures shall still be removable otherwise it becomes the property of the owner of the property.

The answer is **(C)**

Solution 164

Attachments are anything attached to the property and can be classified as either natural or man-made. Natural ones are living things such as trees, shrubs, or flowers. Man-made ones are installed and not a naturally occurring element of the property.

The answer is **(C)**

Solution 165

The bill of sale is proof of a transfer of ownership. However, a bill of sale may either be absolute in which ownership is transferred entirely or conditional in which the grantor has a conditional claim to seizure if stipulations are not met.

The answer is **(C)**

Solution 166

Land has four distinct economic characteristics that influence its value as an investment:

- Scarcity
- Improvements
- Permanence of investment
- Location or area preference

The answer is **(B)**

Solution 167

It is important to note that the assessed value for a property is not the same as the appraised value. The assessed value, along with the millage rate is used in the determination of the property taxes.

The answer is **(A)**

Solution 168

Both police power and eminent domain are forceful means of taking property from a homeowner in which an agreement has not been reached. One of the key differences is that eminent domain does require some compensation to the homeowner whereas police power does not.

The answer is **(B)**

Solution 169

Zoning ordinances set restrictions on how a property can be used or modified. Most often, they are determined at the town or city level of government for a specific region.

The answer is **(C)**

Solution 170

Eminent domain may be used for a portion of a property or an easement and it is not necessary to obtain the entirety of the property. If it is determined that the project is for the good of the public, eminent domain may be used to obtain the necessary easement.

The answer is **(C)**

Solution 171

Community property is joint ownership by a husband and wife during their marriage in which each spouse owns everything equally, regardless of who earned or spent the money. This is not available in all states.

The answer is **(D)**

Solution 172

Fee simple absolute is an interest in property a person will receive when they either buy land or receive land as a gift. The interest is absolute because the interest will not end on the occurrence of an event or condition.

The answer is **(A)**

Solution 173

The bundle of rights is provided to the buyer along with the acquisition of the title.

The answer is **(D)**

Solution 174

A life estate shall establish a remainderman who is the identified individual that will receive the property upon the death of the life tenant.

The answer is **(C)**

Solution 175

An estate for years is a lease with an established beginning and end date. At the end of the established time period, the tenant is expected to vacate the property, and notice is not required.

The answer is **(A)**

Solution 176

A gross lease is one that includes all costs a tenant might incur during their stay. In addition to rent, this includes taxes, insurance, utilities, and any others.

The answer is **(A)**

Solution 177

The title insurance covers both the lender and the borrower from loss or damages resulting from the property title.

The answer is **(C)**

Solution 178

The three guarantees of a general warranty deed include:

- The grantor owns the title free and clear of any defects from the time the grantor owned the property back to prior ownership of the property
- There are no liens or encumbrances other than stated in the deed
- The grantor will defend the title of the property against third-party claims

The answer is **(B)**

Solution 179

Avulsion is the sudden loss of land by natural processes. This may occur due to events such as hurricanes, landslides, earthquakes, erosion, and others.

The answer is **(A)**

Solution 180

A marketable title may not be free of mistakes but a court will legally force its acceptance by a buyer.

The answer is **(C)**

Solution 181

Many states require an attorney to provide a closing protection letter which is an additional certification by the attorney who issued the opinion of title. It certifies the information provided and assumes responsibility for any legal recourse that could arise due to erroneous reporting.

The answer is **(B)**

Solution 182

The characteristics of value include:

- Demand
- Utility
- Scarcity
- Purchasing Power
- Transferability

The answer is **(B)**

Solution 183

Flipping, which is commonly confused with house flipping by a contractor, is when collusion occurs between a buyer, appraiser, and a lender in which a home is bought and then sold artificially for a higher price in a short time frame.

The answer is **(B)**

Solution 184

The right to receive notice must be provided within 3 business days.

The answer is **(A)**

Solution 185

Depreciation is only taken for work classified as an improvement and not repairs. A roof falls under improvement and can be depreciated. The yearly depreciation is the cost of improvement divided by the lifespan:

$$Yearly\ Depreciation = \frac{\$7,500}{10} = \$750$$

The answer is **(B)**

Solution 186

The property tax is determined from the assessed value of the property and the millage rate or mill rate. The mill rate is expressed per $1,000 with one mill representing $1 in tax for every $1,000. Therefore, to find the property tax, multiply the assessed value by the mill rate and then divide by $1,000:

$$Property\ Tax = \left(\frac{\$220,000\ x\ 26.5}{\$1,000}\right) = \$5,830$$

The answer is **(B)**

Solution 187

A CMA should take into account any features of the property that may be determined to affect the value. Fireplaces, landscaping, and scenery are all relevant choices.

The answer is **(D)**

Solution 188

A gross income multiplier is calculated by dividing the property's sale price by its estimated or provided gross annual rental income. Therefore, to determine the rent from a targeted gross income multiplier use the following:

$$Gross\ Annual\ Rental\ Income = \frac{Sale\ Price}{Gross\ Income\ Multiplier} = \frac{\$600,000}{5} = \$240,000$$

Since this is the annual income, we can find the monthly income by $120,000/12 = $10,000. Then since there are five units, the rent per unit is $10,000/5 = $2,000.

The answer is **(B)**

Solution 189

Economic obsolescence is a loss of value of a property due to factors that are external to the property. The catalyst is outside of the control of the owner of the property and therefore the issue can most likely not be corrected.

The answer is **(D)**

Solution 190

The reproduction method determines cost from an exact replica of the property including original materials.

The answer is **(C)**

Solution 191

For investment properties or landlords, costs for work performed on a home can be depreciated but must be classified as a repair or improvement. Improvements are more substantial and permanent including renovations, additions, and remodeling. Repairs are work done to fix portions of the home due to wear and tear. This would include plumbing work to a single sink.

The answer is **(C)**

Solution 192

Consideration ensures that some level of value must be exchanged for a contract to be binding. The value does not have to be at some minimum level of adequacy for the contract to be executed but some value must be present.

The answer is **(C)**

Solution 193

An unenforceable contract will not hold up in a court of law and eliminates any obligations imposed on parties in the contract.

The answer is **(D)**

Solution 194

Recission is the legal removal of obligations from parties in a contract. The court determines that the parties shall be returned to the point of obligation as if the contract was never executed.

The answer is **(B)**

Solution 195

The statute of frauds mandates that for a contract to be enforceable it must be in writing and be signed by the person against whom enforcement of the contract will be sought.

The answer is **(A)**

Solution 196

The earnest money deposit is binding as soon as the agreement is communicated between the buyer and the seller.

The answer is **(C)**

Solution 197

A financing contingency allows the buyer to look for and obtain proper financing to complete the purchase of a property. If they are unable to, the contract can be terminated and earnest money returned.

The answer is **(B)**

Solution 198

A general agent establishes a representation of the client for a range of activities under a specific purpose. A property manager handles more than a single transaction but is still limited to the scope of the properties.

The answer is **(A)**

Solution 199

Implied agency involves actions taken that a reasonable person can assume agency has begun. The declaration of intention and the discussion of properties implies the intention of agency.

The answer is **(B)**

Solution 200

Once agency is created with a client, the agent is held to certain legal responsibilities during representation of the client. These include:

- Care and diligence
- Loyalty
- Accounting
- Obedience
- Disclosure
- Confidentiality

The answer is **(C)**

Solution 201

There are three options upon receipt of a counteroffer: accept it, reject it, or make another offer and continue negotiations.

The answer is **(B)**

Solution 202

The seller concessions are limited to a percentage of the sales price based on the down payment amount. For a 5% down payment, the limit is 3%. Therefore 3% of $250,000 = $7,500.

The answer is **(D)**

Solution 203

As a part of seller financing, the seller remains in possession of the legal title until the buyer pays in full. This allows the seller to foreclose on the home if payments are not made as per the agreement.

The answer is **(C)**

Solution 204

For an option contract to be established, it shall contain the premium, the purchase price, and the timeframe in which the buyer must decide to exercise the option.

The answer is **(C)**

Solution 205

A renter pays a security deposit but it is still owned by the tenant until there is a determination that it needs to cover repairs or some other applicable costs. Until that time the landlord shall keep the deposit in an escrow account and any interest is owed to the tenant.

The answer is **(A)**

Solution 206

Section 1003.3 covers exemptions from the need to report. Section (c)(2) indicates that unimproved land need not be reported.

The answer is **(B)**

Solution 207

The Good Neighbor Next Door program allows these types of professionals to seek discounted properties in specific areas.

The answer is **(C)**

Solution 208

HUD approved counselor's help with services related to the ability to pay a mortgage for a borrower. There is no HUD hotline, however.

The answer is **(C)**

Solution 209

The title report may be obtained through any means desired by the purchaser. It can be done personally at the assessor's office or courthouse but most often it is obtained through a professional.

The answer is **(D)**

Solution 210

Public information for complaints includes the date, subject, and a description if consented. There is no mention of penalties, but the resolution of the complaint is indicated

The answer is **(D)**

Solution 211

Title III of the ADA prohibits entities that own, lease, or operate a place of public accommodation from discriminating against the disabled. The ADA requires equal access and services to disabled individuals in the most integrated setting possible. Architectural and communication barriers are to be removed in existing facilities where such removal is readily achievable and can be carried out without much difficulty or expense.

The answer is **(C)**

Solution 212

The GLBA provides guidance to institutions regarding the sharing of non-public information. They must at a minimum disclose:

- What information is collected about its customers
- With whom the financial institution shares the information
- How the information is protected
- Opt-out options

The answer is **(A)**

Solution 213

Calls can be made no later than 9 pm.

The answer is **(C)**

Solution 214

Debt to income is a measure of the monthly debt obligations to the gross income, not the net pay.

The answer is **(C)**

Solution 215

If a borrower is delinquent there is a number of actions that can be taken by the lender. A short sale is when the lender agrees to sell the home for less than what is owed.

The answer is **(C)**

Solution 216

Acceptable reasons are related to the applicant's inability to display creditworthiness but may also be related to the proposed property. Common circumstances for denial may include:

- Poor credit history
- Insufficient assets
- Proposed property having unfavorable characteristics
- Lack of employment history
- Poor credit score
- Immigration status

The answer is **(B)**

Solution 217

Redlining is the unethical practice of not providing services to residents of a certain area based on race or ethnicity. The Community Reinvestment Act in 1977 was passed to prevent these practices.

The answer is **(C)**

Solution 218

General liability insurance cover costs related to bodily injuries and property loss or damage.

The answer is **(D)**

Solution 219

Price fixing is an agreement on a standard set price across multiple companies.

The answer is **(A)**

Solution 220

If there is no insurance on a property due to reasons such as failure to pay, the lender can force insurance on the borrower so that the property is still protected. This is known as force-placed insurance.

The answer is **(C)**

Solution 221

The Clean Water Act (CWA) regulates discharges of pollutants into the waters of the United States and establishes quality standards for surface waters.

The answer is **(B)**

Solution 222

The 1992 Residential Lead-Based Paint Hazard Reduction Act required anyone licensed individual involved in the sale, lease, management, construction, or appraisal of a property built before 1978 to provide a clear notification to parties involved in the transaction.

The answer is **(D)**

Solution 223

Phase III is used when contamination has already been identified. The tasks will include determining the extent of the contamination and developing a remediation plan.

The answer is **(C)**

Solution 224

Some of the health concerns with certain substances include those which can become airborne and therefore pose a significant respiratory risk. This is indeed the case for all of radon, asbestos, and mold which will release contaminants that can be breathed in.

The answer is **(D)**

Solution 225

Flood zones are geographic areas that FEMA has classified according to varying levels of flood risk. These zones are depicted on a community's Flood Insurance Rate Map (FIRM). The zone a property falls in determines the requirement for flood insurance. Those in high-risk areas are required to have flood insurance. High-risk zones include:

- Zone A
- Zone V

The answer is **(A)**

Solution 226

Loan flipping is when a borrower is encouraged to refinance without any real benefit. This results in unnecessary additional fees and costs.

The answer is **(C)**

Solution 227

The up-front mortgage insurance premium is a closing cost specific to an FHA loan and cannot be avoided regardless of the down payment amount.

The answer is **(D)**

Solution 228

A construction-only loan is actually two separate loans: one solely for the construction of the home and then a mortgage. Because of this the fees for the loans are separate and require two sets

The answer is **(D)**

Solution 229

The attorney fee cannot be charged by the lender and is not allowable.

The answer is **(B)**

Solution 230

Despite the fact that a loan may have the necessary equity to remove PMI, if it is not absent at the origination of the loan, there is a seasoning period in which the borrower must wait to apply to remove the payment. This period is a minimum of 2 years.

The answer is **(B)**

Solution 231

For an application to be received and complete, it must include:

- Consumer name
- Consumer income
- Social Security number
- Property address
- Estimate of the value of the property
- Loan amount sought

The answer is **(A)**

Solution 232

A decrease in a fee does not count in the cumulation of recording fees. Only increases are counted.

The answer is **(A)**

Solution 233

Any changes that are needed after consummation may be made in a revised closing disclosure within 30 calendar days.

The answer is **(C)**

Solution 234

Points are a way to pay an up-front amount that will lower the interest rate on a loan. Each point is worth 1% of the loan. In this case, 2 points will cost $6000.

The answer is **(B)**

Solution 235

The return on an investment (ROI) is the ratio of the net profit or loss upon sale of the asset. Return on investment is often indicated as a percentage:

$$ROI = \frac{Net\ Return\ on\ Investment}{Cost\ of\ investment}\ x\ 100\%$$

The net return is all of the income associated with the property:

$$Net\ Return = \$20,000 + \$5,000\ x\ 5 = \$45,000$$

Then calculate the ROI:

$$ROI = \frac{\$45,000}{\$350,000 + \$10,000}\ x\ 100\% = 12.5\%$$

The answer is **(A)**

Solution 236

Appreciation is the increase in value of an asset over time. Appreciated value is calculated by

$$Appreciated\ Home\ Value$$

$$= Sales\ Price\ X\ (1 + Yearly\ Rate\ of\ Appreciation\ (Decimal))^{Number\ of\ Years}$$

Therefore, the estimated property value after five years is:

$$\$200,000\ x\ (1 + 0.03)^5 = \$231,855$$

The answer is **(C)**

Solution 237

The IRS has the following exemption amounts for net profit from a sale for an individual filer:

- $250,000 of capital gains on real estate

The proceeds are the net gain minus the existing payoff of the mortgage. The net gain must account for the closing costs. Therefore, the gross gain on the property is 95% of $350,000 which is $332,500. The seller is allowed a net gain of $250,000 so the existing payoff must not be less than $332,500 - $250,000 = $82,500.

The answer is **(A)**

Solution 238

For PMI to be avoided, typically the down payment needs to be 20% or more. Therefore 20% of $200,000 is $40,000.

The answer is **(D)**

Solution 239

Per diem interest is calculated by taking interest on a daily basis. The equation is:

$$Daily\ Interest = \frac{rate}{365}\ x\ prical\ x\ time\ period$$

$$Daily\ Interest = \frac{0.0425}{365}\ x\ 242000\ x\ 30 = \$845.34$$

The answer is **(D)**

Solution 240

Monthly payment = 820 + 1200/12 + 6000/12 + 82 = $1502.

The answer is **(B)**

Answer Key

1	A	41	D	81	D	121	D	161	C	201	B
2	A	42	C	82	A	122	A	162	D	202	D
3	C	43	B	83	A	123	D	163	C	203	C
4	B	44	C	84	D	124	A	164	C	204	C
5	C	45	C	85	C	125	B	165	C	205	A
6	C	46	C	86	A	126	C	166	B	206	B
7	B	47	D	87	B	127	D	167	A	207	C
8	A	48	A	88	D	128	A	168	B	208	C
9	C	49	A	89	C	129	A	169	C	209	D
10	A	50	A	90	D	130	C	170	C	210	D
11	C	51	A	91	D	131	D	171	D	211	C
12	B	52	C	92	B	132	B	172	A	212	A
13	D	53	C	93	C	133	C	173	D	213	C
14	C	54	D	94	A	134	D	174	C	214	C
15	B	55	C	95	D	135	B	175	A	215	C
16	C	56	A	96	D	136	A	176	A	216	B
17	B	57	D	97	D	137	C	177	C	217	C
18	C	58	D	98	D	138	B	178	B	218	D
19	B	59	A	99	A	139	B	179	A	219	A
20	D	60	A	100	B	140	C	180	C	220	C
21	B	61	D	101	C	141	A	181	B	221	B
22	B	62	B	102	B	142	C	182	B	222	D
23	B	63	A	103	C	143	A	183	B	223	C
24	C	64	C	104	C	144	B	184	A	224	D
25	C	65	B	105	D	145	B	185	B	225	A
26	C	66	D	106	C	146	C	186	B	226	C
27	A	67	B	107	D	147	B	187	D	227	D
28	C	68	D	108	D	148	B	188	B	228	D
29	A	69	A	109	B	149	C	189	D	229	B
30	C	70	B	110	B	150	B	190	C	230	B
31	D	71	D	111	C	151	A	191	C	231	A
32	C	72	A	112	C	152	A	192	C	232	A
33	C	73	A	113	B	153	A	193	D	233	C
34	B	74	C	114	B	154	B	194	B	234	B
35	D	75	B	115	A	155	A	195	A	235	A
36	A	76	C	116	C	156	B	196	C	236	C
37	A	77	A	117	D	157	B	197	B	237	A
38	B	78	A	118	B	158	B	198	A	238	D
39	C	79	A	119	C	159	B	199	B	239	D
40	C	80	D	120	C	160	A	200	C	240	B

Thank You Again for Your Purchase!

What Did You Think of the Study Guide?

It is a long and difficult road to passing and we are extremely grateful you chose us to help along the way. We hope that it added value and efficiency to your studying. We are here for any questions or concerns you may have and we will respond quickly if you email us at:

Bovabooks@gmail.com

If you enjoyed this book it would help greatly if you have the time to **leave a positive review on our Amazon product page**. Reviews help to support small businesses like ours.